brendan
NEILAND
on reflection

brendan
NEILAND
on reflection

In conversation with Cathy Courtney

To Jack

with all best wishes

and my thanks

Brendan Neiland

Jan 2000

MOTIVATE
PUBLISHING

Published by
Motivate Publishing

PO Box 2331, Dubai
United Arab Emirates

PO Box 43072, Abu Dhabi
United Arab Emirates

Macmillan House
96 Kensington High Street
London W8 4SG
United Kingdom

Directors:
Obaid Humaid Al Tayer and Ian Fairservice
Publishing Manager:
Catherine Demangeot
Editor:
Kate John
Art Director:
Dejan Vrbanovic

First published 1997

ISBN 1 86063 025 1

British Library Cataloguing-in-Publication Data.
A catalogue record for this book is available from
the British Library.

Printed by Emirates Printing Press, Dubai.

To Bryan
1943-97
brother, aide and accomplice

Contents

The material for this book is based on the National Life Story Collection's Artists' Lives recording with Brendan Neiland. (The recording may be heard at the British Library's National Sound Archive.)

Foreword

I have always felt that a challenging ambiguity lies behind Brendan Neiland's work. At one level, his paintings are images of things made, and of materials and their properties, particularly of transparency, reflectivity and the absorption of shadow, memories culled very often from his own perception of architecture. At another level he explores the hard edge of technology that can seduce with its precision. One of my favourites among his paintings, *Waterloo International*, vividly represents these qualities by translating into the work the feeling of place, and the presence and sense of arrival that the architecture of the new station creates with its crystal roof, that covers and encapsulates a piece of central city.

  Neiland discovers in architecture something which is uniquely pictorial. Following in a long, painterly tradition, he looks in a formal and accessible way at buildings and man-made components of cities, and the order underlying them. His paintings and contribution are important in making us look again, and in a different way, at this aspect of our physical surroundings and the technology with which we construct the world; above all, on the questions that this raises for us as human beings.

Sir Philip Dowson CBE, PRA
President, Royal Academy of Arts

A Moment of Tranquillity

Architecture is generally static; if a building is moving, then either we call it something else (a ship), or we assume that it will become properly a building only when it stops (a caravan). The representation of buildings in photography and in paintings is, one might assume, of the still life variety. Film and video can certainly inform about the activities which take place within a building, and indeed distort the building, but as to the bricks and mortar themselves...

In his paintings of architecture, however, Brendan Neiland adds an extra dimension to the mediation which takes place between architect/building and painter/observer: time. The reflections which form a central part of this aspect of the artist's work have a timelessness which derives from the fact that they are particular moments, captured initially through photography, then transformed into something which is at once two and three-dimensional: the experience of seeing the photograph of the painting is very different to seeing the painting itself.

In each case, we see either a permanent structure which is reflected in a more temporary medium (the image in the lake), or an image of a moving element (a cloud) captured in the reflective surfaces of the building itself. This apparent tension between movement and stasis, reflection and absorption, becomes in Neiland's work a moment of tranquillity; it is not work which evinces anger, lust or laughter, but contemplation and (non-visual) reflection. It is perhaps not so surprising that he spent some time living in a monastery.

If architects too rarely think about time, they certainly think about other matters which concern Neiland as a painter: light, layering, the collapsing or modification of form through visual distortion (the crude example of which is to be found in the funfair Hall of Mirrors). The idea of the façade and its relationship to nature, its environment, other buildings and the viewer is a subject to which contemporary architects have returned again and again. The way in which glass is used: to reflect, to protect, to make itself invisible, to welcome, to reject, find echoes in Neiland's work. What is it that makes one see a building as an anonymous city office block, or a 19th-century railway station? Could they be reversed? When we see the church spire reflected in the glass, are we seeing something old or something new?

The techniques involved in Neiland's 'moment-capturing' are relatively new, and like any technology, especially in the hands of an artist, will generate their own aesthetic. Even given the technology, however, reflection is a difficult trick to pull off; in Neiland's work it is achieved with an ease which one realises can only result from painstaking effort and attention to detail.

In the end, the power of the work comes from the knowledge that the still image of the painting implies both movement and life beyond it. You might turn away from a cloudscape, turn back and think you were looking at a fresh image; clouds are all different and yet the same; reflections are all different yet they have much in common. You might say, certainly of the architectural works, that Neiland has produced an artist's notion of frozen music: listen and it melts.

Paul Finch
Editor, The Architects' Journal

From Meditation to Practice

Childhood

Although I was born in Lichfield, most of my childhood was spent in East Anglia, mainly in Swaffham, Norwich and Lowestoft, a part of the English countryside that, particularly in those days, was rather remote. My brother Bryan and I had bicycles and used to pedal out to the dunes and beaches, and go swimming from Easter onwards – even though it was cold – or we would go out climbing trees and scrumping for apples and peas. It seemed an endless time of boisterous and joyful activity and, in that sense, my early life was one of tremendous freedom.

As much as I loved the quietness of the countryside, I also loved the bustle and activity of Norwich, which was the first city I explored. It had a market on Fridays and Saturdays, selling fruit, vegetables and livestock. As we were growing up, my brother and I were frequently taken to Norwich Castle and Museum, where the paintings by Cotman and Constable made a lasting impression on me. The landscape Constable painted was very obviously the one I lived and walked in, and I am not sure, looking back, whether I was aware of the landscape through nature itself or through looking at Constable's paintings. The experience of rowing all day on the Norfolk Broads was rather like stepping inside his pictures; in a boat on that special stretch of water I was tremendously aware of being low down alongside the long, straight line of the flat landscape, with the strength of the sky and huge clouds pressing down above it. The drama lay in Constable's work whereas Cotman's was more to do with drawing and had a finer, quieter beauty. Many years later, when I became an artist myself, the work of Cotman and Constable gave me the confidence to paint clouds as the sole subject of my paintings.

As well as visits to the Museum, I enjoyed the cathedral at Norwich; although it was decaying and needed restoration, it was still magnificent and had a lovely aura to it. I have always been fascinated by the smells of churches – by their archways and doorways, the windows – and many of the East Anglian examples go back as far as Saxon times. I was brought up a Catholic and we went to Sunday Mass and Benediction and the Stations of the Cross but, despite that, my understanding of Catholicism was pretty minimal as a young person. One vivid experience of my adolescence was a pilgrimage I and the other altar boys made with the parish priest and some visiting French children, walking from Norwich to Walsingham, which is about 15 miles. From my point of view it was an adventure rather than a significant religious experience; it was only later that religion became a way of life.

I have no memories of drawing until I was in my second year at Lowestoft County Grammar School. By chance, the husband of my English mistress ran the Art Institute in Lowestoft, and she thought a painting I had done of a moon coming through clouds was good enough for me to go to Saturday classes at the Institute. Not long after that, one had to make decisions at school as to which subjects to specialise in and, probably at my parents' dictate, art was relegated although I carried on at the Institute on Saturdays.

A lot of the paintings I did at this stage were based on the Norfolk and Suffolk skies: The East Anglian countryside gave me a yardstick against which I could

measure my experience when I went to Dartmoor and the Lake District or the Western Highlands of Scotland in adult life. Each of those places has a unique quality that I relate to against the landscape I absorbed when I was growing up.

One Christmas, when I was 13 or 14, my parents bought me a collapsible easel and oil paints, and I shot off in the freezing cold to the harbour and sat and painted the trawlers and drifters and the fish market. Although I no longer have them, I remember these paintings as having a soft quality, stemming from the yellow lights that the women worked with, gutting the herrings as the fishermen brought them in. When I think back, it is not so much the physical work going on that I remember, more the lights and tents and the shadows that were thrown around; oddly, that relates forcibly to my concerns now.

When I was about 14 the family moved to Birmingham because my father, who was a Civil Servant, had been promoted. My brother and I travelled in the furniture van, which was a great excitement, and I remember passing the spot that marked the centre of Britain. Birmingham was nearby, very much a central city, the home of the motor car and many other industries, with the majority of people there employed in the factories. I loved it immediately. I have had the ideal upbringing because I have the memories of the marvellous outdoor life in the country, and the freedom there, but also the joys and beauties of the city. I get tired of people who complain about urban environments and who wax lyrical about babbling brooks; there is a lot to enjoy, visually and intellectually, in built-up areas. I found Birmingham stunning and went into the centre as much as possible. It was overwhelming and I loved the height, and the fact that you could visit a department store five storeys high – Lewis's – and go to the roof garden and look down on the streets below. It was alive in those days and the city centre was quite different in the late 1950s to how it looks today. Most of the architecture then was heavy Victorian and I found the winter evenings very Dickensian.

I was sent to St. Philip's Oratory School where the curriculum was different, and I found I had to drop biology and chemistry and take up physics and art. I passed the art very well but, again, my parents' influence ensured that I didn't keep it on in the sixth form. Art was not regarded as a future way of life, it didn't come into the reckoning; I enjoyed it but it didn't go beyond that. One day when I was walking up the stairs at school, I passed the art master Tony Sawbridge walking down and he said, "Neiland, why are you not in the art room? You come along straight away. You are going to take the exam." So I became the only one doing lower sixth art and I passed the 'A' level along with the senior pupils that year; and that consolidated my interest. Tony Sawbridge played an important role because he would work on his own paintings while we did ours in the same room; I slightly imitated his style, but even in those days I knew I didn't want to be dominated. I realised, whilst I was in the sixth form at St. Philip's, that I would always be doing art in one form or another. At about that time, I went to see the Birmingham City Art Gallery and was introduced to a

Street Scene – *Painted in 1960 and sold in the same year to the St. Philip's Oratory School, Birmingham, for 3 guineas*

lot of the Pre-Raphaelite paintings there.

It was only when I went to school in Birmingham that I discovered that being a Catholic meant more than going to church and that there is an enormous amount of morality and ethics involved, a whole way of life. I began to acquire knowledge through the school – mine was founded by Cardinal Newman and run by the Oratorians, a very select body of priests. By the time I was in the sixth form I was attracted to the notion of being a missionary priest and it became generally accepted that I would go into the Church. If you had faith and believed, being a priest or a missionary was the most total thing you could do with your life. It was also a romantic idea: I liked the idea of travelling and of the commitment. I had met some of the White Fathers and I remember them coming to visit us and speaking to my parents. At this stage, I was going to church every Friday evening, on Sunday morning and evening and at least once more during the week.

The Seminary

I left school in 1960 and that summer took the boat to Ireland and the train to Enniskillen and then caught a bus, before beginning a two-mile walk with my heavy suitcase. The Seminary was at Blacklion, a border town in the middle of nowhere, between Enniskillen and Sligo, and I remember how beautiful it looked as I approached. It nestled in a slight valley between two gentle mountains, a new building containing around 60 cells – simple rooms with a bed, a table, a light and a sink – as well as the chapel, lecture rooms, a common room, the dining-room and the kitchen where the French nuns cooked.

As I was to find, it was a rigorous life at the Seminary and the Order accepted that there would be a high drop-out rate – the intake for my year was about 30 and we were fully aware that it might be that only one of us would be made into a priest. The day would begin at six o'clock when a bell would be rung and someone would rap on the door and say something in Latin, to which you had to reply, to show you were awake. There was no further talking until after breakfast. You had half an hour to get ready for Chapel at six-thirty, where you would meditate until seven and then there would be Mass and Thanksgiving. Between seven forty-five and eight-fifteen there would be physical exercise – swimming or running – so you were mighty hungry by eight-thirty when breakfast was served. A book was read aloud, in either Latin or French, during the meal and then we would go straight into four one-hour lectures, studying the history of the philosophy of the Catholic Church.

At twelve-thirty we would have had a break and were allowed to talk, and those who smoked could go outside; it was infrequent that you could speak, but pleasant when it happened. Then there was an hour or so when you either laboured outside on the farm or did domestic duties inside the building. Then there was a period of intensive study as at least once a term we had examinations that we had to pass; I admired the Order for the fact that priests had to be of a certain intellectual level. At five o'clock there was a tea-break and then another period of study, after which we would troop downstairs and the Father Superior would give a talk. There was an evening service in the

Chapel, a late supper, community recreation and then bed at about ten o'clock.

Whilst I was in Ireland I did no end of painting, probably more than I had done in my life until then – religious pictures, cards and also stage-sets for plays that we put on for the locals on feast days – and I was also writing a bit. Getting praise was not part of the training to be a priest – it was just accepted that I was the artist and did the art – but the Order was supportive in using talents and recognised them quietly as a gift, whether it was being good at Gaelic or football or having a beautiful voice. I did a series of Mother and Child paintings and another series of Christ on the Cross and other religious subjects. (I also did a self-portrait in a cassock and Roman collar, looking rather like a stern, Calvinistic version of Adolf Hitler.) One thing I did that was unique was to develop a form of large mosaic, shaping heads of the Madonna and Jesus Christ in coloured sawdust on the walkways of the Saints' Day processions. In a sense it was a forerunner of environmental art. I would chalk up the designs and then scatter dyed sawdust to form these huge religious icons, possibly 10 feet in diameter, which meant standing on a ladder to get the perspective right. As the chanting procession walked over them, the images would disappear underfoot. I was part of the procession and remember the quality of the young men's voices singing plain chant, and the wonderful sense of the sound being held in the air between the mountains. One expression the Irish have is "Ah, it is a soft day." Softness does describe Irish landscape for me, even the mountains. My whole remembrance of Ireland is a gentle, slightly filtering rain or brisk, blue days.

I suppose my idea of the appearance of God and the Saints was very much dictated by the religious art I had seen, the Fra Angelicos and Michelangelos. I had first been abroad when I was in the sixth form at school, and early on went to see the El Grecos in Toledo, the Goyas and Velasquez in the Prado and all the religious paintings in Italy. As a Seminarian, I was lucky to be able to stay in the Vatican City and see the rich collection there. I remember seeing a Raphael painting in the Vatican with grids or bars as part of its structure, and I often think of that when I am painting my own grids. Obviously, the Sistine Chapel was stunning and we were particularly lucky in being taken around it early in the morning when there was no-one else there. On the same visit I must have walked round almost all the three hundred churches in Rome, too. Whenever I went abroad – and I began to travel as much as I could – I would do watercolours and drawings every day. Sadly, I kept none of these, which I regret now.

I went through a lot of trauma whilst I was with the White Fathers and found the life very difficult. If the Seminary had been on the mainland I might have left sooner, during one of my many periods of doubt and despondency, but I idolised the Father Superior, who was a good mentor for me, and he would have been hurt if I had gone. You can have doubts regularly in a Seminary. As soon as they occurred, you went to the Superior or to your personal priests and told them about it; by the end of half an hour, of course, you felt the Grace of God back in you, and you went to the

1960 - With my brother Bryan (right) at Blacklion Seminary, Co. Cavan, Ireland

1962 - Self-portrait

Chapel to thank Him for showing you the Light and the Proper Way. In the end I stayed in Ireland until the end of the first two-year period when there was a natural break, which may have been a coward's way out. At the end of the second year, the next step would have been to enter the White Fathers proper, wearing the white garments, and spending a year in the Novitiate in England. Faith is a peculiar thing; the fact that in the end I didn't have it has turned out to be a good thing for me.

The experience at the Seminary was formative and not at all wasted. I don't think my life has changed because I elected not to become a priest. From the outside it is different because I am no longer a Catholic and am not even a Christian, but the dedication that was required for the priesthood is exactly the same dedication I am now giving to my art. I don't wear a cassock or a white collar and I have a spray gun and a mask for my face instead, but other than that, the way I apply myself is very similar indeed. The activity may be different but the total commitment is still the same.

Birmingham College of Art – Foundation Year

At the end of my two years in Ireland, I got in touch with the Principal of the art college in Birmingham and said I wanted to leave the Seminary and go to art school. I joined the Foundation Course, based at Bournville on the outskirts of the city, in September 1962. It was slightly odd adapting to life there after the Seminary; for instance, it took some time to get used to the fact that people referred to the tutors by their Christian names, but the college was fairly traditional at that period. Picasso was still thought of as a strange man who did peculiar paintings of cut-up women. At the Foundation School the staff were tenacious painters, interested in skill and dexterity and the students were expected to do still life and figure compositions. Even though I knew I wanted to paint, I had to do a bit of photography, a bit of furniture design, a bit of ceramics, and I was soon bored to death doing them. It was a time when people who were unsure about which path they wanted to follow could try different things, but all I wanted to do was get back in the painting room. I remember the day when the model first came into the room naked; that was a tense moment. Other than in a painting, I cannot recall that I had ever seen a naked female. All of us were studying our paper and pencils. We drew everything but the breasts and pubic hair. I remember drawing her watch and then the time on her watch. But we soon got over that. Life drawing is good experience, not just as a discipline, but as an activity in itself. It is important to see and work from something you are observing. You are abstracting and putting down marks on a piece of paper and making them have significance. You are putting down a statement. In the first few weeks, it was a matter of getting to grips with observed drawing and realising how difficult it can be.

During the year, I and four others wrote to the Principal saying we were going off to Paris to broaden our view of the world and our artistic integrity. We

1961 - Deposition, *Oil on board (10 x 7.6 cm)*

Birmingham, 1962 - Factory Study, *Pastel, charcoal and pencil on paper (41 x 48 cm)*

15

went off in our duffle coats and unshaven locks and bare feet, and took a look at St-Tropez as well as Paris. It was all part of growing up. It had a huge impact on all the other students because it was such a romantic ideal to follow. Fortunately, I had quite an impressive demeanour in those days and when the Principal took me into his office on our return he said, "You should not have done this, but under the circumstances, we will let it pass."

The only important fruit of that Foundation year was the life-drawing work, apart from gaining some understanding of colour theory from a tutor who talked to us about the Bauhaus and colour relationships. However, whatever I produced was good enough to get me onto the next part of the course at Birmingham College of Art, which was based in the centre of the city.

Margaret Street Painting School, Birmingham School of Art

When I went to Birmingham, the courses had just changed radically. I was fortunate in some respects to join at the point when the old National Diploma in Art and Design was ending, as it had been a very strict, structured course where students had to pass certain examinations and show ability in being able to draw from a model, to put figures in a particular composition and to paint in various ways. My course, what is now the BA but was then called the Dip AD (Diploma in Art and Design), was free in the sense that you could do virtually what you liked. That does not necessarily train you to become a good academic painter, but it did allow us a phenomenal breakthrough, and we were probably lucky in still benefiting from the overhang of the discipline of the previous generation. No actual practice or manner of painting was taught so you found your own route, which is why it probably took me longer to discover the right direction for myself.

The head of the College was William Gear who, through the years, became very important to me, mainly because of his kindness and support. His studio was in the College and it was interesting to see a living artist at work. The door was always open and he would say, "Come on in, boyo" in his Scottish accent. It was a smallish room with a big easel and not much else. Bill always had time to listen; he would go on working while you spoke to him. He was a genial, kind man and was underrated by the English art establishment, but he remained optimistic and held no bitterness or grudges.

New staff had been brought in to teach the course, so we had John Walker, Trevor Halliday, Allan Miller and Ivor Abrahams, all young and enthusiastic with tons of energy. They made us much more aware of contemporary art and of what was happening in America, of Abstract Expressionism and Pop Art. All the time they were teaching us, they had in the back of their minds the great steps forward that painting was taking, from Jackson Pollock and Rothko to Auerbach, all sorts of movements that would, ultimately, influence us. Ivor Abrahams gave me his first tutorial in a pub, which was shocking and affected my life ever since because it was the first time

1961 - Mother and Child, Oil on board (10 x 10 cm)

Birmingham, 1962 - Factory Study II, Pastel, charcoal and pencil on paper (32 x 44 cm)

I had had a drink in a pub.

Ivor had an enormous impact on me. I spent a period in the sculpture department and made a horrible piece that looked like a plaster dalek. Ivor talked about understanding form and about facets of form. I could not grasp what he was talking about, it was a foreign language. I know more now, but it is something that comes to you with maturity and age, rather like a philosophical statement. He was trying to tell me that I didn't have to have a smooth round surface, that it could be made up of facets. I was amazed. He was intrigued by my being so naïve and yet so keen; he could see that I was struggling and wanting to learn and he questioned me so that, without giving me any answers, he gave me some clues as to how I might mature.

As far as painting was concerned, we were thrown into a six-week course based upon moving figures, which broke down all our barriers and any traditional manner of looking. Not only did we have our own works, but we looked at other people's and altered them. Ivor Abrahams pointed out that, left to ourselves, everyone stood at 15 paces from the model and never came forward to look or work from a different angle, which showed a great lack of ingenuity. We watched him go up with a pair of callipers and measure the distance between the two nipples of the model without any fear or trepidation, and after that we were a lot freer; although we didn't go and touch the model, it broke the ice. Another thing the tutors did was give us sheets of paper five-feet high, which could be fastened together; they were trying to break down our inhibitions and to stop us looking and drawing in a representational manner. Maybe that is why the subjects I work with now are caught between abstraction and figuration.

As well as working with paper, we worked on hardboard, with collage, with emulsion, with charcoal. We were encouraged to get 6-inch, 12-inch brushes as well as 2-inch and smaller. The work became gestural, the input of the whole body. On one occasion, we were taken to the Lickey Hills on the outskirts of Birmingham, and worked for two weeks in the snow from morning to dusk. It was an atmosphere of intense light and dark, emphasised by the shapes made by the snow and the gaps in between them. It was easy to make marks across the paper that had little to do with the trees themselves, but a lot to do with the snow camouflaging them which had created something different again. Each evening we had to take the work into a hut for general criticism. Later, I built a three-dimensional piece based on this experience, using hardboard, chicken wire, papier maché and plaster. I built shapes reminiscent of rolling hills and gaps in the snow.

All the activities I have described took place in the first two terms. At this time we each had a screen or a large canvas and were just told to paint it. I slapped the paint on, not having the faintest idea what I was doing and I didn't like the result. It changed my attitude and by the end of my first year and for a lot of the second year I worked out of the college, in my studio at my flat. It gave me a freedom away from the strong determination of the staff. I made a lot of mistakes. At one time I worked for about five months in the Botanical Gardens and got more and more involved in close-up views of particular plants; there

1965 - Machine Study, Pencil on paper (24.7 x 19.5 cm)

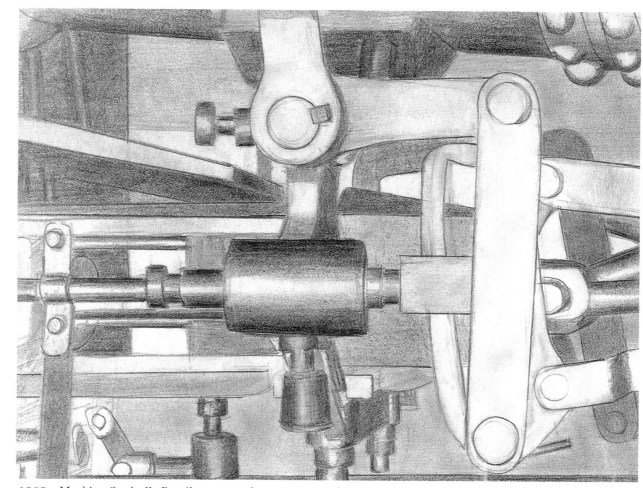

1965 - Machine Study II, Pencil on paper (19.5 x 24.7 cm)

17

was an enormous amount of squirming on the canvas. I took the paintings to college and asked the tutors for criticism and got absolutely slated, decimated. They were very unkind. I got up the following morning determined to show them what I could do. The time that followed was when I began to develop.

The influential Léger

I was very conscious of wanting to work with particular subject matter. I was asking myself what was Birmingham about? Why was it called the centre of Britain? I began visiting parts of the city I had never been in before, like the car factories. I got permission to work in one of the factories at Bromsgrove where they were smelting down 60-ton ingots and turning them into sleek, high-finish propellors for boats; I spent about six months there, drawing every day in pastel, pencil and charcoal. I also obtained a weekend job (mainly because I needed to earn some money) working as a guard for Securicor. I would go to a factory on a Friday evening and stay until Monday morning. The loneliness was extreme and it was frightening in such a huge, empty place, but it meant I could spend time with all sorts of machines. I used to put the power on and see how they ran, which was slightly dangerous because I knew nothing about them, but it gave me the opportunity to look at metal cutting and other equipment in action. I would spend the rest of the weekend drawing and drawing. The machine parts were the oddest of shapes and these became embedded firstly in my drawings and, when I gained more confidence, in my paintings.

At the same time I was looking around for artists who might have used contemporary imagery and I discovered Léger. When I first saw his work I thought it was repulsive, crude and ugly – particularly his treatment of hands and feet – and it didn't appeal to me in the least. I disliked the paintings so intensely that I felt there must be something there and I kept looking at them in more and more detail. Later I made the connection between his paintings and the drawings I was making from observing machines. The repetitive simplistic form he used to describe fingers – the sausage quality – was not dissimilar to the mechanical forms and shapes I found within the Birmingham Science Museum and factories. Once my eyes were opened, my sense of affiliation with Léger grew and grew, until I came to adore his work, I virtually ate it in my studio.

I talked about Léger to the historian who taught us art history and he suggested that I write to Douglas Cooper, the great collector of Léger, Picasso, Braque and Gris, and ask if I could go to see him because of my special interest. I dropped Cooper a line and received a flamboyant postcard written in green ink saying that if I were near Avignon at any time I should come to visit him. I went with my girlfriend, and we drove and drove, until we came to his house, which had the remains of a Roman colonnade and villa in its garden.

Cooper was quintessentially English, with a blazer, trousers and cravat, and he was delightful company and very welcoming. He spent four hours with us and showed us his private collection of over 140 works. The Légers were disappointing but the Braques and the Gris were stunning. He spoke freely of his association with them all and, in that way, opened my eyes considerably. One thing I remember him saying was that none of them lived in a garret, drinking cheap wine and eating only bread and cheese. They all lived well and had all the equipment they needed, as well as good studios and terrific meals. Ever since then I have seen no reason why artists should not own part of the world; I don't mean only in monetary terms because money alone does not make a rich life, but food, drink, company, studio, lighting and other equipment – all those are necessary. However, that was not the only revelation that I got through Cooper, it was exhilarating to be with someone who was still seeing Picasso almost every day. We looked in the visitors' book and Picasso's name was on virtually every page.

Cooper told me that Léger was a little apart from the others. Whereas Gris and Braque and Picasso were always in their studios, Léger much preferred the company of factory workers and a smaller band of people who didn't associate so readily with other artists. My one regret is that we didn't go to meet Léger's widow. That was Douglas Cooper's fault because he said "She has nothing to offer. She would be wasting your time." I cancelled my appointment with her. Looking back, I realise Cooper was probably jealous of her because she knew Léger more intimately than he did. We did, however, go on to the Léger Museum in Biot, which was extraordinary, so much work.

Maybe I saw in Léger a tutor whom I was lacking at the Art College. I felt ignorant and in need of education, visually, structurally and fundamentally. In the room I worked in I had reproductions of his paintings alongside my own studies from the factories and the Science Museum. I created a series of paintings using his colours, his structures and my forms. I never copied a Léger, I would have found that too boring, but I made a series of transcriptions using his palette of simple reds, blues, greens and pure whites, and I tried to emulate the rhythm of colour that flows through the best of his paintings. Again, the cleanliness of his black outline was something I liked and used to describe the forms. I also did a number of drawings of my girlfriend very much using Léger's methods; I love the women he painted reading, or languishing or in a machine environment.

The process became very real – I went to the museums and factories and brought back the material, but using it alongside Léger's manner of working gave me something to relate to and believe in, an individual, personal foundation. I realised there was a future for me through the forms I was drawing, although I could not quite understand what it was at the time; I could use the forms as a kind of hieroglyphics which became meaningful. The studies I made in the factories and in the Museum were of specific parts of different machines – for instance, I was fascinated by the shape of a cog and the teeth working with it or the mechanics of a piston – and I amalgamated them to form compositions for my paintings. They didn't represent elements that would be able to function together in reality; they were machine environments. I needed to find a way into painting for myself and I worked through Léger for at least two years. I even carried him with me at the beginning of my time at the Royal College.

1970 - In my Shepherd's Bush studio

The Royal College of Art

At the Royal College I continued rather as I had done at Birmingham. I had begun to introduce some of the colours I had seen at the factories, the warm colours from the furnaces and the surprisingly delicate colours that coated the finished machine parts despite their massive size. There was an extraordinary scarlet and an ultramarine blue that had particularly impressed me with their starkness and originality, and it had been compelling to discover such colours within the grime and grot of the factory environment. Those industrial surfaces pushed me in a different direction to the one which I would have anticipated, in the sense that they revolutionised my approach in terms of the tools I used.

Towards the end of my time at Birmingham, I had realised that although the quality of paint I wanted on the canvas could be achieved with a brush, it was, firstly, extremely hard work and, secondly, it looked unnatural and unpleasant. Since I was after a smooth surface, like that of the finished machine-parts, it occurred to me that the air brush that was used to coat the metals would be the logical thing for me to try. Within a month of arriving at the College, I ordered a compressor and, although Carel Weight, the Professor of Painting, said he didn't want any mechanical means of painting in his School, he did nothing about it when it arrived. (In fact, after I left, Carel ordered a compressor on behalf of the College!) That sort of openness to the changing desires and needs of the students was the great strength of the College.

During the months when I was waiting for the compressor to arrive, I decided to do some serious life drawing with a static model. I wanted a change. I needed to make a break with the Birmingham work and I was wise enough to understand that although there was a lot of strength in my interpretation of Léger, it was not the way forward for me. I needed to re-assess my thinking and my art. Within a day or two spent in the life class I realised the way the rest of the students were drawing wasn't for me; everyone's work was adept and had a fine, very delicate line, but my experience of drawing in the factories made me want more solidity. I had a different attitude and, although I carried on drawing in the same room and from the same model, I tore up my early attempts and set off on a different path. I wanted to discover the body and mould it, bring it out of the paper.

What I did next was a series of four or five charcoal drawings that took up to three weeks each. After my initial frustration, I relaxed and ended up enjoying the series. The model was lovely, slightly heavy, not plump but with plenty of body to her, and brownish in colour. I spent six or seven weeks working from her, on the flesh and the folds. I must have spoken to her, but I don't remember it. It was quite private and tense on my part and the drawings took a heck of a lot out of me, but I knew they were working and that I was achieving something – solidity – that I really wanted. Working from observation, I was able to put down my feelings in a personally expressive manner, to portray the physicality of the body and its pressure against the folds of the mattress.

With Financial Times *Art critic Bill Packer and Roger de Grey, past President of the Royal Academy, in the garden at Crépé – 1991*

Surrounded by some of the works produced while at The Royal College of Arts

Eventually the compressor and air brush arrived; I was very happy; although I had had no experience with them, I had a gut feeling that they were going to be the right tools for me and they were. I was able to achieve exactly the finish I wanted and I never used the brush again, other than for preparing surfaces. I was content at this stage to use the forms from the factories and museums – I had by now begun to visit the London Science Museum, too – and I went to local factories and collected catalogues and bits and pieces. A car-spray business gave me a thrilling colour chart and I was looking at industrial finishes more and more, allowing them to influence my work. I was painting mainly using Indian ink with the airbrush, working flat on a table so that the ink would not run. The approach was much more freehand than it later became and the drawing was less complex than it is now. I did hundreds of small drawings in the first and second years at the Royal College. It was an exploration.

At the same time as making the drawings with the spray gun, I was building three-dimensional pieces. It is a part of my career that I prefer not to remember, but it related to the machine parts. One piece was a kind of arch that came out from the wall and stood off the ground, made of hardboard and fluorescent light, and painted blue; it appeared to be rising from the floor. This kind of building took month after month, preparing, sanding down, painting, rubbing down, repainting. I also made a number of repeat shapes that interlocked, but they didn't have the quality of intellectual visual input that I wanted. This type of work took too much time and I ultimately found the pieces inflexible and limited. In retrospect, I was a little influenced at this stage by the American painter, Jim Dine, who was a visiting tutor at the College, and I remember admiring a show of his that used hundreds of images of saws and hammers and pliers. In the same way as I enjoyed Dine's use of everyday objects, I was caught by the work of Rosenquist and Wesselmann, who made spaghetti and lipstick, cars – anything – the subject of their paintings. I remained very affected by John Walker, too, and the way he used shapes, and I had been much engaged by a show of Larry Poons which had ovaloid shapes rushing over his canvases.

Whilst most of the forms I was drawing were derived from machine elements, some were tubular and one series in particular made use of a car exhaust. I began looking at photographs of American cars and their engines and became more and more intrigued – again I was examining bits and pieces rather than looking at the whole unit. My images were based on the component shapes, and I would stick them onto a piece of plain paper, trying to see whether the forms were significant enough to be made into shaped canvases or three-dimensional pieces. I was in a quandary. I didn't know where they were leading, but I didn't want to force the work in one direction rather than another. The great asset I had at the College was time. I have always believed that as long as I am painting and drawing and in the appropriate place, something will happen in the end; an artist builds up a knowledge of the subject he or she is dealing with. The work of this period simply existed. Some of it was ugly and should not really have been done, but it all helped me to think.

The Minories - Colchester, 1972 with Lucy and Naomi. They have made an enormous difference to our lives. It was wonderful growing with them, experiencing things through their eyes, helping them read, swim and ride, to say nothing of being presented with their stunning drawings. The family is indescribably important. I feel no division between family life and my working life. Having my studio in the house has meant Hilary and the girls have always witnessed the paintings as they evolve and I always listen to their comments, which are always honest and open. They have got nothing to lose and they are happy to be part of it all

Two of the more complete pieces were selected for the 'Young Contemporaries Exhibition' and were bought by the Contemporary Arts Society. They were the beginning of the lead to somewhere else. One was of drill bits against a reflective metal surface which reinforced the cutting edge and mechanical quality of the drill. It was the first time I remember using a reflective surface and although it was a turning-point it was accidental. I remember wondering about how I should use the backgrounds of the paintings and realising the reflective surface of sheet metal pleased me very much; I didn't immediately make the connection with car surfaces.

Spurred on by the excitement of success in the 'Young Contemporaries', I carried on working until I came to a point – probably around Christmas of my third and final year at the Royal College – where the collaged objects on top of the reflective surface became almost incidental. I had moved on from thinking of sheet metal surfaces simply as backgrounds, to considering them the subject of the work itself: the background had become the foreground. I began to concentrate fully on the highly-finished sections of car bodies, a transition which had the additional advantage that, although there were fewer of them than there are today, cars were familiar to virtually everybody as a form of imagery in publications such as 'The Sunday Times Magazine', and viewers would feel at ease with them. My upbringing in terms of the legacy from Birmingham had been with the Abstract Expressionists and my natural tendency was towards abstraction, but I still preferred a figurative source.

By using the familiar reference point of the car as my starting point, I could carry the viewers towards abstraction almost without their realising it. I was rather tired of the esoteric quality of some of the abstract painters and the way they were so removed from the general public. I didn't want to be alienated, I wanted to communicate with people at the same time as satisfying my own needs.

Up until this point I was still working on paper whilst all the students around me at the College were painting on canvas. I remember one of them saying to me around this period, "Are you not yet ready for a canvas? You must start painting properly." I could not think of a reason why not. I immediately made a canvas, 11 feet by about 4 feet and worked on that. After that I was able to jump in scale considerably – the images on paper had been about two and a half feet by a foot – and I went up to 12 and 15 feet quite quickly and without a problem. Not only did the imagery deserve the larger scale, but I also wanted the panels (as I thought of them) to be environmental so that it took the viewer a few seconds to pass by them. I didn't want dinky things framed on a wall.

The changed scale of the work brought about another development because I began using a spray gun with the compressor instead of the air gun, so that I could respond better to the sweep of the surfaces I was tackling. I worked on one wall at the College and I would spray heavily onto the canvas. Where shapes or edges had to be determined, I would cut out bits of paper on the floor and then fix them onto the canvas with masking tape and spray against them. In some

respects it was a much more immediate way of painting than the way I approach it now. If the colour was too dark, I would spray white on it, whereas nowadays I colour mix and build up with controlled glazes.

The hard surface of the car imagery was something I had been subconsciously preparing for almost from the early days of working with Securicor in Birmingham. The three-year period at the College was an important apprenticeship that I was privileged to have. I was forming a grammar, a body of forms and shapes which I knew would serve me (and probably still do recur in my work), at the same time as I was also becoming adept in the means and technique that would hold the future for me. Birmingham was a terrific foundation, but the time at the College matured me and set me at the beginning of the route that I would follow in the future.

While I was at the Royal College, I met Hilary Salter, a painter who had trained at Goldsmiths, and we married in 1970. I have found our relationship and her support absolutely critical to my development as an artist. She has without doubt kept me sober and painting. I left the College having been awarded the Silver Medal and the John Minton Travel Scholarship. All the paintings I hung for my degree show sold. Everything seemed to be at my feet.

My former tutor Ivor Abrahams (second from right) with (left to right) Evelyn Abrahams, Brad Faine, his father-in-law and Hilary in our garden in France, 1993

1992 – At home in London on my birthday with Naomi, Hilary and Lucy

Working Methods and Materials

1977 - Using masks in my London studio

Soon after I graduated I was working on a 30-foot canvas, *Sunset Bonnet* (page 52), that was included in the exhibition 'Large Pictures for Public Places', which was curated by Carel Weight and Roger de Grey, who was Reader at the College, for the Royal Academy in 1969 and was shown again at the Whitworth Gallery in Manchester in 1971. It was at this point that my contact with Daler-Rowney began because they were developing a new form of paint, Cryla Flow Formula, which I think was the first time acrylic was available in this country. It was due to be marketed in competition with oils and they asked if the Royal College painters would try it on our big paintings before they launched it on the market. Ever since then their paint has been at the core of my work, although I also use Liquatex and Aquatec. When I told Rowneys that I wanted to spray with their paint, they made a mix that was more amenable to being used as a liquid, and they were also open to suggestions about developing colours according to our growing needs. I can trust my paint, I have grown up with it and known it for a very long time.

I will colour mix before starting a painting, which is time-consuming and wearing, but fundamental to any piece of work. I have got thirty or so lidded pots and I will go through a range of colours that I intend to use, either spooning the paint in or putting it in in brush loads. It is worth my while to have as much paint around as possible as I certainly don't want to run out while the work is in progress. Mixing the paint is instinctive. I will be trying to get as rich a range as I can, within the limits chosen for the individual painting. To a certain extent I know what my colours are going to be when I dabble them into my pot and begin mixing, but the longer I go on working, the more my understanding deepens.

I use a relatively heavy canvas, 15-ounce cotton duck, which has a richness that I enjoy. I was brought up at Birmingham to make my own canvases and stretchers and, early on, I remember looking behind a Larry Poons canvas at an exhibition and finding it was the best stretcher I had ever seen and resolving that I would always emulate that. It is important to me to stretch the canvas myself because, through moving around it in the process, I gain an innate understanding of its size and scale. The stretchers are made of 3 x 1 wood, planed, with half-inch beading attached to the edge. The beading makes them distinct and detaches the canvas from the wood, without which (because of the manner in which I paint) the mark of the wood comes through onto the surface. My stretchers are tough and strong, which helps give body to the finished work, and I have got all the tools I need – hammer, chisel, plane, nails, pins, nuts and bolts, screwdriver and drill – many of which date from my Royal College days. I have always believed that whenever I earned money from the paintings, half of it should go back into the 'business' so I have made sure I had all the professional equipment necessary. There were a group of us at the College who very much pushed each other on towards a professional attitude, which was wholly beneficial.

Once the canvas is stretched, I take it into the garden and put the hose on it to wash out the impurities. I let

1974 - The difficulties of this painting, which I was working on when Naomi was born, resulted in drawn masks. I stopped using masking tape

it almost dry and then, as I always work on a colour base and never on white, I brush on a coat of colour that will relate in general to the image that I am going to develop. It is a system that has been used by artists throughout the ages – Rembrandt, Goya and Vermeer often worked against coloured backgrounds – and it has been my practice since I left the College. Again, I will let that almost dry and then apply another coat and build up layer after layer until I have got quite a body and vibrancy of paint. The weave of cotton duck is not as fine as canvas – I like to have some tooth in it, an edge – but by the time I have put on six or seven coats in preparation, it is an excellent, and at times succulent, surface to work into. Later, as the painting develops, some of the areas are pure paint and you can no longer see the canvas. Other areas, in contrast, still have some quality of the weave to them.

For many years now, I have used a system of paper masks to assist me as I build up each image. These allow me to concentrate purely on the particular section on which I am working at any one time whilst effectively blocking off the rest of the surface and keeping it clean. While waiting for the various preparatory layers of paint to dry on the canvas, I will be cutting the paper to size on which the drawings for the masks will be made; the paper on which I will draw will be slightly bigger than the canvas. The drawing stage is crucial to the understanding of a painting as it is the masks which help dictate what the final result will be. The mask drawings will be taken from my drawings on site and from photographs I may have taken, and any other information that I feel is right. Usually, the general drawing will be transferred onto 10 or 12 sheets of paper masks, each of which will be cut so that I have an edge against which to spray each area of colour; because I am not using a brush but still need the distinction a brush will give, I employ the edges of the paper and the holes to achieve that distinction. In the process of making the masks, I come to know the structure I am dealing with much better. All the drawings will be laid out in my

second studio and together – not in any special order except in terms of the various lights and darks that will be used to build the highlights – they will allow me to construct the whole painting.

I vividly remember when I invented the idea of the drawn paper masks and stopped using masking tape. It happened whilst I was working on a painting representing a sweep of buildings reflecting clouds, at the time my daughter Naomi was born in 1974. Up until then I had used the tape to cut off areas that needed to be kept free from whatever particular colour I was spraying. It would take me two or three days to mask off a complicated area and the problem that then arose was that I would have no idea how well or otherwise the new colour related to the area covered by the masking tape. Three-quarters of the time, when I removed the tape, I would find that the two colours didn't work together and I would have to start the process all over again. In this particular painting there were a lot of soft areas surrounded by the taut structure of the building. The building section would be taped off so that the cloud areas could be developed but it was severely restricting to have such a fixed separation and, once I had thought of the paper masks, I never looked back. My style of drawing will often depend on how I am feeling; sometimes I get terribly tight and measure everything, sometimes I am relaxed and free. Certain paintings need a definite, tight structure, but there might afterwards be a lot of free hand and eye work on top. I have exhibited the masks both at the Tate and the Whitworth Gallery, in order to explain the make-up of a print or a painting, and sometimes the masks are arresting to look at in their own right.

Once the basic structure is decided, it will not alter during the creation of the painting, but within that there can be any number of changes in terms of increasing or decreasing emphases and darkening and lightening hues. It is only in the development of the painting that you become aware of what you are looking at. A lot of the process of painting is looking and making decisions; it is not just doing. You go into

1987 - Working on Lloyd's *print*

the studio and believe that you have got to do this painting. It is something you have got to say, to experience, to discover. It is personal. My paintings work on an emotive level and on a very solid structural level; I am trying to do the two things in one. I will always do my very best to make sure it is successful and that it works. That is in my nature. I have never had any doubts.

I tend to spray heavily so I work flat, partly to avoid runs. Even though the paint is acrylic, left to its own it would take half or a quarter of a day to dry, so I have a heater and two hairdryers which I play over the surface until I can carry on working. I can use whatever pressure I want to control the air coming through the spray gun and this dictates the size of the dot which hits the canvas; the less pressure, the bigger the dot. Where necessary I work into wet paint, but I like to ensure that I am fully in control and that I don't get any streaky qualities. If I want a soft effect, I will lift the mask up and bleed the spray. If, for instance, I am building up the centre of the painting to a white, I will bring in another mask and, while the underpaint is still wet from the previous spraying, I will put on the white so that it fuses with the colour underneath. I rarely use a paintbrush – I don't require the interference of the brushmarks – but I use my

fingers and hands a lot. The masks give me a lead, but I will use any means to get the result I need.

My London studio is in the basement of our Victorian family house in Clapham, South London; it is a good-looking building with superb proportions to the rooms. After seven years at art college, I wanted to be away from the interference of sharing a space with other artists, but having a studio in our home meant I could see my daughters in the evenings and read them stories at night as they were growing up.

The studio is three-quarters underground but has French windows at one end which open onto the garden and one large window in the second room which faces the road. I work in the garden room and use the cleaner space to keep my large mask drawings. The floor is lino, now covered in paint. In London I use fluorescent light, colour-balanced tubes and I have them on whatever the brightness of the day dictates. Most of the museums and galleries show by artificial light and, as long as the light source is constant, this suits me well. I learnt a lesson about light years ago, when I had a studio in Shepherd's Bush, shortly after leaving the Royal College of Art. I was developing a canvas with very intricate areas and I worked overnight and discovered in the morning that this had had a disastrous result because the yellow of the

1990 – At work on one of the InterCity *paintings*

I remember seeing a Polish film while I was at the Royal College and the film-maker said, "The most delicate tool of all is the little finger." My hand is a very delicate tool where my paintings are concerned

artificial light had affected everything I had done. The lesson was that I had to paint by one light, either natural or man-made, preferably in the same space.

In the middle of the studio I have a rickety old drawing table; it is easier to work at that height than at floor level. One of the most important tools in the studio is the compressor, which is still in the original box in which it arrived at the Royal College of Art. It is a DeVilbiss, the Rolls Royce of compressors, basically an engine with a tank, from which a hose leads to the spray gun. The compressor is about three and a half feet tall and I lay my spray gun and two brushes and rags to clean the gun on the lid. There is a bucket of water nearby. I generally clean up every evening; although it is not a pristine place, it is ordered.

I have colour charts on the wall; Aquatec and Rowney's Flow Formula, and all the paints I am currently using will be grouped together near the mixing buckets. After years of painting I am not necessarily able to articulate what colour I am after, but I will know which pot to dip into to achieve it. I usually prepare canvases against one particular wall and that tends to get covered in whatever base colours I use, so it is a miniature history of my painting since 1971, the year we moved into the house. The walls are otherwise white and get refreshed every few years. I don't keep past paintings in the studio, so the walls are bare. No painting is ever finished, you just reach a stage where, at the present time, you can do no more to it. If I had old paintings around, I would keep thinking I could move some detail or increase or decrease the elements, so I prefer my gallery or the person who has commissioned them to take them out of the vicinity, to stop them affecting my vision of the next canvas.

My easel is a particularly splendid example. It came as a consequence of my *Waterloo International* commission (page 124). The painting was a focal point of the opening ceremony of the new station and it needed to be on an appropriate and solid stand, for the moment when the Chairman of British Rail unveiled it. I and one of the site architects went to Rowney's and bought the sturdiest easel we could find, a wind-up affair on four wheels. British Rail had no use for it after the ceremony so I was very happy to have it, both for practical purposes and as a reminder of that moment. I don't actually paint on it, but it holds paintings of all sizes and I put them up there when they are dry, to have a look at them off the floor.

I have a pneumatic seat in the studio, which I use only occasionally when I am drawing and never when I am painting. There is also a filing cabinet with my personal papers and a good chunk of my photographic library. Brad Faine, my printer and print dealer, gave me a trolley and that holds the weights that I use to press the paper masks down on to the canvas, little bits of lead borrowed from a printing workshop. The trolley also holds an Egyptian cat – I think it is lucky – that my wife, Hilary, gave me as a birthday present, and below that is a television, in case I need to replay the cricket. I have got an excellent sound system and I usually listen to music or to cricket commentary on the radio while I work. On one of the speakers sits an Indian god, a beautiful statue.

My palette – The colours mixed for Autumn [1997], *the painting above*

My studio in France, at Crépé, near La Rochelle

Buying the house in France, near La Rochelle, was motivated partly by family needs but partly because I don't like to spend any time on holiday away from work. My studio there is beautiful. It has large windows in the roof. The sun beams straight down so I can always work in daylight there, unlike London. It has two huge wooden doors that open directly onto the large country garden, so it is almost like working outside. This one is taller than the London studio, perhaps 25 feet high in the middle, and I love that kind of space around me.

In the part of France where we have our house, the colours have a great richness and intensity, and I suspect the colours in the paintings I do there absorb some of those qualities too. When I am there, I work by natural light and stop at seven or whenever dusk settles. If I haven't time to complete a painting in France, I will do the preparatory drawings there but I will not begin it until I am back in London.

I have never had an assistant in the studio because I like growing with the paintings, all of which can shift and change at every stage. I like to work in stretches of about five hours, with total concentration and no interruptions. The intensity of it is wearing and it takes a lot out of me, but I need the passage of time to manipulate and play, to tease out the changes and to create. You cannot dictate in a dispassionate manner, you must allow the painting to grow as your own awareness and understanding enlarges. I make each one work by minute adjustments, going from the general to the particular, and, if there is a danger in the work, it is in playing with the subtleties and allowing them to overshadow the underlying elements.

It is important to have ideas for the next painting before you finish the first; whether you follow through that particular idea or not does not really matter. I have had super ideas that have never gone on canvas or paper, partly because I have gone beyond them in my head. Often, the following painting will be in slight contrast to the previous one; if I have worked on a very structured canvas, I might follow this up by doing a looser one, perhaps with a lot of clouds or some freer areas.

I don't anticipate radical changes although there have been important shifts in the past. I started with factory images and was led through this to reflections, and from there to the reflective qualities of car bodies. Through the subject matter of the reflections in the cars, I became more aware of my environment and its meaning, and that became more and more central to my creativity. I look back at my history of painting as embodying a greater awareness of my surroundings.

You have got to be very tough to be an artist. You have got to be selfish and determined. But it is incredibly pleasurable. What a terrific thing, just to be able to create! And to create what is important to yourself! I would hate not to have enough in me to carry on painting and I would be frightened if I stopped. If I am not working, I feel guilty. When you are young there is so much excitement. As you get older, there is so much you want to do and the years are running through quite quickly. On one level, my philosophy and attitude is one of trying to come to peace with myself and I'm searching for an equilibrium and calmness. Life is amazingly complex and I try to make a simplicity with my paintings. There is an enormous amount I want to do in the future.

Working on the Hackney Community College painting, Shoreditch Church and Waterloo

Printmaking

Working at Coriander Studio, London

Printmaking is about a tenth of my working life. My creativity is developed more often through paintings, but I usually do two or three screenprints a year as well, always working with Brad Faine of Coriander Studio. We have worked together for 20 years and he is not only someone I trust as a professional colleague, but he has also become a close personal friend. It is an important relationship because a print is a collaboration, the only time in which I'm not operating entirely independently to achieve the final image and ensure that it succeeds. Brad and I have the shared objective of trying to make the best possible print using whatever number of colours we've decided on. I value his judgement and comments and he fully understands what I am aiming at.

Skyscape - mask being lifted revealing one of the separations

The first print I ever made went badly wrong and I learnt a lot from it. I worked with Brad in the studio and spent about a month building up the sky area, knowing that I was going to add a dark building against it. I reached a point where the sky was superb, but it had become so subtle so that it almost disappeared when I put down the near-black building. It was a great shock. After that experience I developed a new method and will now come back to the studio and make drawings – possibly 10 or 12 separations on acetate. These separations are used to form the screens from which the colour is built up on the print; the smallest number of screens we have worked from is probably 6 but on the bigger prints we might use as many as 22. It is, of course, possible to have blends of colour on a screen, so the potential becomes very diverse.

Nicholas Savage, Curator of Prints & Drawings at the Royal Academy of Arts, looking at my prints in the Academy's permanent collection

It is very exciting building the print up, and the separations themselves are sometimes beautiful. Over the years I have become better at understanding what the colours can do on a screenprint – it is quite different from using them to paint with – and, like many artists I tend to work quite directly with the process. It is still an art form that I have not totally mastered, and since I would need to work full-time in a print studio, I have no intention of doing that. I like the idea of having a fellow artist collaborating with me and I am always surprised that both names are not on the final print. Without Brad Faine, many of the prints by major British artists would not exist.

Brad and I like to put one or two prints into the Summer Exhibition at the Royal Academy. We will meet to discuss the format and ideas behind it – a lot of the images I have done with him have been buildings in the City, such as Lloyd's, but more recently we've moved – alongside the paintings – into landscapes and cloudscapes.

1997 - With Brad Faine discussing the future Four Seasons *prints in Crépé, France*

I use my camera as a sketchbook

Photography

One of the reasons I use photography a fair bit is that the imagery I use changes so quickly. Another is that I always had people coming and looking and chattering to me if I stood and drew, which was awkward. I like to have privacy when I'm working from the outset. A lot of my ideas are held photographically. I have got an extensive range of photographs of all sorts and sometimes their significance will not come to me until years later. I use photography and I like looking at the results, but I don't like holding the camera or taking photographs, which is odd as it is so important to the manufacture and construction of my work.

I am not interested in any aspect of photo-realism or photo-reproduction. If the idea is there in a photograph, I develop it, but it is my vision and visual reaction that is important. Similarly, I am not interested in arriving at details on a building which can be mathematically determined or which make literal sense. I am not in the slightest interested in whether they could be developed further by an architect or a mathematician. My ambition is to make the painting feel right on the canvas and that often requires enormous artistic licence.

Galleries

1971 - With Angela Flowers and her Gallery artists

1987 - With Lloyd's *at Fischer Fine Art*

1997 - With Richard Selby, Maggie Thornton and Richard Gault of The Redfern Gallery

The Royal Academy of Arts, London

Angela Flowers Gallery

I left the Royal College in 1969 and joined the Angela Flowers Gallery in 1970. Angela was full of life and it seemed an extension of life at the RCA, highly enjoyable on all levels. The paintings in my first show with the gallery were a development of the College days. They all sold and for a quarter of an hour after learning that, I felt elated. Then I realised that part of my life was gone and I had no paintings. Everything depended on the next painting, not the ones that had gone before. I have always felt that.

Fischer Fine Art

I moved to Fischer Fine Art in 1978 and the initial show for them was based almost entirely on my experiences in New York, which I'd first visited in that year. Fischer's was a wonderful gallery and I felt comfortable there and protected.

The Redfern Gallery

When Fischer's closed, I felt attracted to The Redfern, which is an old-established gallery, very honest and direct, and which I joined in 1992. I have worked closely with Richard Selby and, particularly, with Richard Gault, with whom I have travelled in the Middle East several times. I have total trust in both of them, which is essential in any relationship. It is crucial for an artist to have the confidence that a gallery has a belief in his or her paintings, and is steadily working on their behalf. I need the protection that a gallery offers, and I consider myself to have been fortunate with all those I have been with.

The Royal Academy of Arts

Roger de Grey, who was one of my tutors at the Royal College of Art, went on to be President of the Royal Academy. The Professor of Painting at the College, Carel Weight, and Leonard Rosoman, another tutor, are also distinguished Academicians. Traditionally, there are only 80 Academicians (and often there are fewer) and so it is only after a member dies that a place comes free. After having taken part in 'Big Paintings for Public Places', the exhibition Carel and Roger organised in 1969, I had no formal connection with the Academy for several years. However, in the 1980s, Michael Rothenstein and Peter Blake proposed me for election and I duly became a Royal Academician in 1992, which is something I am proud to be. The fact that artists of the calibre of Alan Jones, Eduardo Paolozzi, Ron Kitaj, John Hoyland, Patrick Caulfield, Sandra Blow and Joe Tilson are members encouraged me; it feels very much part of the contemporary art scene. It represents a broad band and I view myself as someone on the cusp of figuration and abstraction.

The Story of a Painting

National Bank of Dubai [1997]
Acrylic on canvas, 183 x 122 cm

25.3.97

The National Bank of Dubai is a splendid building, the work of the internationally renowned architect Carlos Ott. It rests on the side of the Creek and its design is based on a dhow. The sail part is the bowed glass that bends out as though it is going to reach over the Creek; it is also quite thin, so it is silhouetted against the sky. The reflections of the Creek and the sunset or sunrise and the passage of the sun are quite extraordinary. The possibility of painting the building has been in my mind for a year. I saw the building in its early stages. It is now almost complete on the outside and I am waiting for the inside to be finished. I have been given two possible sites where the pictures will hang within the building. Instead of doing a large painting for each, I have suggested doing five which would look at various aspects from both outside and inside the building. I anticipate that I will use the Creekside for at least one of the paintings, probably in a fairly abstract manner, to get the feeling of the water and the shimmer of the architecture.

26.5.97

I have returned to Dubai for 10 days and seen the site where the paintings are to hang. A decision has been made that there should be three and I have decided they should be the same size to give a unified sequence to the reception area, where they will hang. At this stage, I am drawing and thinking and drawing. I will be doing an exterior using the Creek and the building itself, which I have started. The other two will require a return to Dubai in early September.

The last trip enabled me to consolidate my ideas on the first painting, and to build up the information I need in drawings and photographs. I had every intention of spending from sunrise to sunset on the opposite shore to the Bank and at times it was so hot that I was barefoot in the Creek. Although it was 110°C, I forgot the heat and stood waiting and looking, until I got burned. I got up at five o'clock one morning and took a taxi across the Al Maktoum Bridge to the other side of the Creek. Another day I spent between ten in the morning and four in the afternoon there. The following day I was there between four in the afternoon and seven in the evening. What threw me unexpectedly was that, because of the humidity and dust, and the position of the sun at this time of year, the real golden sunsets that I remembered no longer occur. What I saw this time was much quieter with none of the bravura and strength of the previous visit, and since I want to use the golds, black greens and yellows that I had seen on the earlier visit, that is a problem I have to solve. I have all sorts of records, so I am not too worried.

The extra days on site gave me greater confidence in the beauty of the building and all its powers. It is amazing, after all the looking and thinking, to get down to the pencil and paper and brush. A relief. I am putting down the structure for the first painting and then I will play with it later. I am really pleased I have started.

3.6.97

The canvas for the first painting has now been stretched and then hosed comprehensively in the garden to tighten the material and remove all the creases.

The image I am working on will be the front of the building, with its façade reflecting the Creek and the golden sunsets. The canvas, almost dry now, has been coated many times with a golden ochre and this provides me with a base on which to work. I have seven sheets of paper – the masks – larger than the canvas, on which the drawing will unfold. I am beginning to imagine a brilliant deep blue on the left of the canvas, slashing it from top to bottom, and offering a foil to the whole curved façade. The façade itself and its position on the canvas is basic to the painting, and must be drawn first.

6.6.97

I have decided that the base of the building should be beneath the bottom of the canvas in order to increase the feeling of floating elegance. The drawing has taken several days and is constantly being adjusted, but the time comes to transfer it to the canvas and the real painting begins with all the attendant excitement and angst.

8.6.97

Once on the canvas, the drawing can be tweaked further and after a good deal of looking and asking Hilary's opinion I alter the basic structure by increasing the curve, and am much happier. Now I can begin bringing in the structural lines within which all the dazzling and dancing reflections and rhythms can play. This fortunately does not take too long – it is absolutely necessary but it is the least creative part. I have decided to develop the painting along with the drawn masks, so all the time I have something on the canvas to look at and respond to, the excitement is maintained. Strangely, since starting I have felt fitter, less tired and certainly less hampered by the foot I damaged at Easter. I have no intention of ever kicking another football.

16.6.97

I have regarded the last few days in the studio rather like an unveiling of the canvas. Instead of combining the drawing and developing of the masks, I have decided to work down the façade, putting down a base or general colour. This will give me an idea of the extremes of tonality and also reveal the drawing. The curve is so important.

By the time Richard Gault of The Redfern Gallery arrived on Tuesday morning to take more photographs of my work in progress, the whole of the façade was in place on the canvas. The structure works in an abstract manner and, visually, I cannot detect any glaring errors in the drawing. It is very exciting to see it exist in this manner, waiting for the shimmering nuances – in a way, waiting for my handwriting.

It is frustrating not to be able to spend more time in the studio, but there are benefits; constant looking helps to make it exist and points the way forward. It is a slow process, but absolutely essential. I have invited several friends into the studio and, like Richard, they love it. Someone asked if I had thought of leaving it as it is. No. An artist knows he has to push and to take his canvas further. I have never been seduced by early flattery, but it does breed confidence.

I have a great feeling at this stage. It is going to be a stunning painting. It will not only be a personal response to the Bank but a description of my extraordinary reaction to Dubai, which was, after all, my first entry to the Middle East. I am intrigued and fascinated by the culture and the ambience. Other than the plane rides, I look forward to going back and back.

Time to return to the drawing; this first stage will make the others much easier as the lights and darks fall into place.

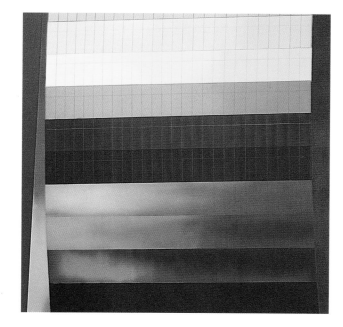

24.6.97

The surface is completely covered. The general colour moves from a cool purple through to yellow golden lights and whites, hit by an area of dark half-way down and by the sparkling lights that I am now teasing into life. The latter lighten the medium-dark areas and relate directly to the water, suggesting a play of light on the Creek. These elements are so important, providing relief from the general colour way down the canvas. This is achieved not only by their tone but also because they are formed from a different kind of mark, bitty and broken, but – I hope – having a rhythm that will relate to the movement and eddies of the water.

The painting has remained static for several days and will do so for a number more. This is not because I have stopped working, but because I am now developing the intricacies of the drawing. This is both complex and very necessary, the nitty-gritty of the painting. The first stage is the general lights; then will come the particular whites, followed by the darks. I am very pleased with the streak of blue contrasting with the browns, golds and mauves. I am beginning to get the feel of heat and shimmer and, through the darks, a hint of dusk.

Now it is back to preparing the drawing for the masks. The painting is already pleasing me, but I must go on to particularise and personalise the image. The weather has changed over the last two weeks, moving from hot, warm days, to rain and generally damp conditions. The paper of the masks grows and shrinks. Still, it is a growing painting!

I have been listening to the cricket commentary (weather permitting) on the wireless as it provides a wonderful background. I tend to play music or have the radio on, as I need that kind of company or sound in the background, but I might be working away and not even know what I have heard.

I love being in the studio looking at the canvas. I want to see what happens next.

36

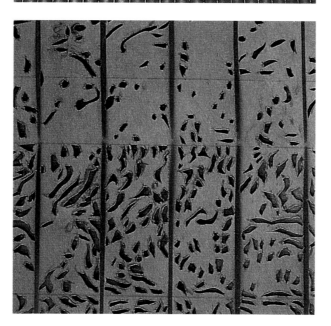

30.6.97

I seem to have spent forever on the eddies and small movements in the water. It reminds me of how surprised I have been at the actual movement in the Creek. As yet, I have never seen it perfectly still. I keep thinking that I might be able to obtain the quality by increasing the spatter dot from the gun, but this seems so random. I think that what I am building up will give that feeling of an almost filigree golden turbulence, not so much a current, but movement in the water.

3.7.97

With Richard Gault photographing again this morning, the rhythms became very apparent. Richard is certain that the calligraphy of the drawing holds a message. Maybe I am fluent in Arabic. Very exciting to see all those days of drawing the minutiae are finally showing their importance. This morning has given me a lot more confidence. This is the area that will give life to the painting and should further enrich the saturated yellow golds.

In the early evening, I drew spacial and structural lines on the marble-clad supports. It always amazes me how much you discover about the buildings through drawing; in this case, the link of line across the windows and through the marble. These are small but critical details. In certain paintings such aspects are unimportant, but in this one they give a unity to the whole canvas.

7.7.97

I am about to start the darks within the water. Towards the end of this week I should be working back on the canvas, developing the water.

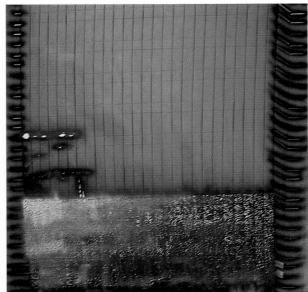

9.7.97

The second day on the darks. Very slow, but when they are complete the canvas should move quite rapidly.

10.7.97

I have finished the linear drawing, defining the marble area. I am now stopping drawing. I need to get back to the canvas to see how all the drawing develops in paint. I will work initially on the water areas that contain all the activity. My palette will stretch from the lightest to the darkest of tones. I shall mix the colours in my pots, keeping them lidded so that the paint doesn't dry out. It is important at this stage to push the tones as extreme as possible. There is always the temptation to be too cautious which means some of the drama could be lost. Part of the purpose of this painting is to bring the outside in, to feel the glowing heat of the sunset through the cool of the air-conditioning.

11.7.97

At last back on the painting. The water with its ripples formed with both lights and darks is beginning to expand. Exhausting day working on quite a small area, but it is a key part of the painting. It brings a different quality to the surface.

12.7.97

Hilary spoke about the painting as a sail blown out by the wind. I am very unhappy with the angle created on one side. It is so difficult to make a decision. The painting of the Creek reflection is brilliant, but there is something wrong with the structure.

This painting is part of my life. I am growing with it. I think about it, dream about it and, most of all, look at it, trying to make decisions. Very odd.

13.7.97

I spent all day redrawing. In other words, repainting the three middle bands of windows, the middle browns and the rich gold ochre. This last one seemed out of proportion from left to right. It must be said that neither Hilary nor Lucy were worried, but once I had noticed the drawing, I had to correct it.

16.7.97

Yesterday I worked throughout on the granite/marble support to the building. This provides the edge to the curve on the canvas. I used the spray gun with a very low pressure to give some texture to the surface – a spattering. Again, I wanted a light area to give extra strength to the blue running the length of the left side.

I gave a lot of thought last night to the hue and tone for the right side. I wanted it dark but there has to be some delineation to accentuate the curve. In the end I used a quiet blue, relating to but having no fight with, the blue already existing. I have decided to bring in a strong, rich blue at the middle centre bottom to bring the eye right across the painting.

I have covered a lot of canvas today and the painting is now almost complete. It is always surprising how quickly things pull together. Something as simple as the line at the bottom of the building makes an enormous difference. I have kept many of the areas simple to contrast with the main spread. In many ways, these sections are framing support and placement to what is undoubtedly the area of interest. In their quietness, they increase and centralise the suggested activity and, of course, they provide relief. The painting, after all, has to work as a totality and when I refer to the abstract qualities this is what I mean: the balance of colour and structure, rhythm and movement over the surface. The small blue rectangle, central bottom, is so important.

17.7.97

Morning

The blue needs to be lighter at the base and immediately above. The line running along the bottom of the building needs to be more steely. This would give more contrast and a slight edge to the general warmth of the painting. I have been fiddling with the blue area all morning. The temptation is to make it less rich – duller – but I am very loath to do this. I want the whole painting to sparkle and have a jewel-like richness. Working on one small particular area, it becomes obsessive, so I have to keep leaving the studio to try for a fresh look on my return.

Afternoon

Well, I have succumbed and added some brown to take down the blue. It was too strong. I am now going to leave that area and look at it periodically over the next few days. I have Fraser McKenzie and Abdullah Saleh coming on Monday to view their commissioned painting. I look forward to their reaction. I have straightened the lines against the dark edge, top right. There is little more I can see at the moment that needs adjusting. I am just going to have to try and see it clearly, to give an objective view about the balances through colour and form. There is always the temptation to fiddle further. I must busy my mind and hands.

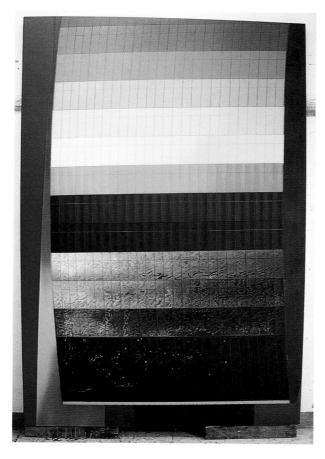

18.7.97

I have shifted the painting into the cleaner drawing studio, so there is no interference in viewing it. It is a strange and memorable image.

21.7.97

Had lunch with Abdullah Saleh and Fraser McKenzie. Richard joined us at the Arts Club. They reacted very positively to the painting – it will certainly be striking on the ninth floor of the Bank.

22.7.97

Richard came for the last time this morning. We completed the photographs of the painting and drawings and, as a final act, I sprayed – as always – my name on the stretcher at the back.

Paintings

Seated Figures [1964]
Oil on canvas, 152.4 x 101.6 cm

Seated Figures was influenced a bit by Cézanne's *Card Players* as well as by Léger, the painter whom I most admired at this period, and who owed something to Cézanne himself. Mine is a tubular painting and relates to Léger in the period from about 1914-20 when he used a lot of tubes to describe his figures and forms. For example, there is a portrait of his where the head is not tubular – it has a hat on it – but the limbs and joints are.

The colours I used derived from one of the first factories I worked in, where 60-ton ingots were smelted. The ingots ended up as high-finish propellers for very large boats, and the surface and finish of them was extraordinary. They were coated in a blue or purple protective coat, very bright and shiny, whereas the colours I used for the painting were blues and purples, but not shiny.

Machine Parts [1964]
Oil on canvas, 101.6 x 152.4 cm

The imagery for *Machine Parts* came from my days working for Securicor, when I spent whole weekends guarding huge, empty factories equipped for manufacturing machine parts. It was a dank, dark, horrible environment but it fed me with extraordinary imagery. As in the other factories in which I had been allowed to spend time drawing, I was excited by the care with which the factory workers maintained the equipment, and by the fact that the dirty surroundings yielded pristine manufactured objects.

More importantly, I was attracted by the oddity and by the innate shapes of the machine parts and these became central to my painting for several years.

As a whole, the arrangement in *Machine Parts* does not make mechanical sense because the various elements are from different structures, but I have used the amalgamation to build a picture which works in its own terms. Every piece and every space has an architectural purpose.

Machine Highlights [1967-68]
Indian ink airbrushed onto paper, 35.6 x 50.8 cm

Machine Highlights was a movement away from the machine bits. I was still open enough to think that a shaped canvas might be the way forward. What put me off in the end was that by making a shape I was limiting myself. I don't like this piece, although the technical side is perfect; in fact the objectivity, the realism of it, was not exactly what I wanted. The painting is not free or open enough. It is controlled, contrived, constrained, compacted.

I would not work with a shaped canvas now. I will have the shape dictated to me by where it is going to hang or by the subject matter.

This painting was based on a solid spring, perhaps a coach spring from an aeroplane or another huge machine. Its source would probably have been a black and white, rather poorly reproduced drawing, and I would have been intrigued to develop it directly and simply. It is the beginning of trying to create a form in two dimensions in a manner that is three-dimensional, and I wanted the image to stand out from the page and be strong. I remember the American painter, Jim Dine, coming round to see it while I was at the Royal College, and we both felt that it would be exciting as an 8 or 10-foot object with the sort of quality and finish I had painted.

This was the heyday of my confidence with the airbrush. It is a simple image and there are not too many complicated areas of spraying, which is probably why it works so well. Once again, the mauve-purply colour relates back to the colours I found in the Birmingham factories. There could have been reflections in this but at this stage I was not aware of them or interested enough.

This image relates back to Léger, the way his objects – an umbrella or a soda syphon, bowls and hands – were incredibly strong.

His were not three-dimensional in manner. I found his paintings quite flat and there was a black edge to them which excited me. Some of his still-lifes have a peace and tranquillity to them that I would relate to Vermeer; Vermeer is a totally different painter but I can see, from my perspective, why I like them both. Léger's manner of painting remains with me to this day and I love silhouetting an object or giving an edge to something so that it has its own identity and power.

There are paintings where I have used shadow almost as a subject matter – it is incredibly rich – but more often than not it will emphasise the actual form I am dealing with. In *Spring*, I have shadow on one side and highlights on the other. I am making the object isolated so that it exists on the page in its purity.

Spring [1968]
Indian ink airbrushed onto paper, 45 x 21 cm

This marks a development for me because it was the first time I was able to use a background powerful enough to counterbalance the machine parts. The horizontal sections relate to one another and give the feeling of motion and activity, and the highlights and reflection increase the sense of the spirals turning. These are strong forms in front of quite a vibrant background. Later, that was to change and I was able to say, "The background alone has enough subject matter. I don't need the presence of these shapes or objects as well."

As before, the crimson, violet and blue related back to my factory experiences in Birmingham quite literally. I was astounded by the strength of them. These were quite small paintings on paper but I wanted them to be powerful and jewel-like, just like the machine parts. I never made this into a huge painting because my ideas moved too quickly and the machine bits themselves became more incidental.

Spiral [1968]
Indian ink airbrushed onto paper, 61 x 40.6 cm

Flow [1968]
Indian ink airbrushed onto paper, 40.6 x 61 cm

High-finish aluminium was a new material at the time I did this, and I chose it as the background. I used the light behind the two forms to accentuate their metallic quality. They are strong, physical pieces placed on a loose, airy, spacious background. It is as simple as that.

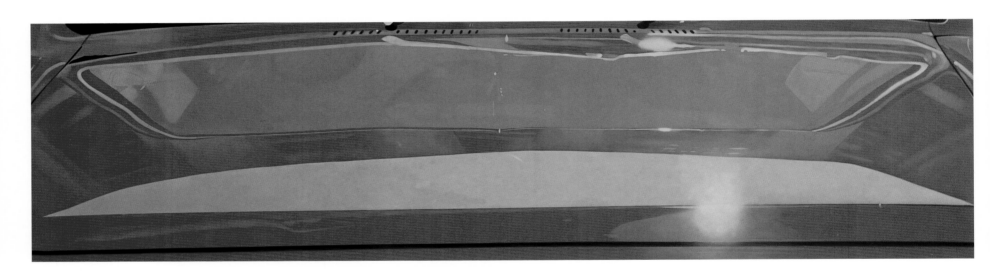

Extended Screen [1969]
Acrylic on canvas, 121.9 x 457.2 cm

This painting is much longer than it is high and I even considered the possibility of it being a free-standing piece. It is based on a red car bonnet, with the windscreen reflected at the top section and a simple, white reflection of the screen below, which occupies almost the entire canvas. The suggested reflected lines of the windscreen wipers are not used to make it more car-like, they are ploys to give movement and positioning within the canvas itself. Even the highlights at the edge of the reflected screen are there to give it an edge, and to keep the eye of the onlooker within the elongated rectangle.

This was an important painting, one of a series that happened in a short space of time, from Easter to my degree show at the Royal College of Art. It was from this stage that I discarded the airbrush, which was making me too finicky. In its place I took up the spray gun and was immediately able to cover more extensive areas. It meant I could work more quickly and more generally, and could extend the imagery beyond small and particular objects. The hand controlled the spray and dictated where it lay on the canvas, and I was able to manipulate the gun so that I could develop areas of detail to contrast with the broader spaces.

My degree show was filled with 12 feet and bigger paintings. Every painting was sold, which was indicative of the times. People were confident and actually bought 12-foot paintings for their drawing and dining rooms. I still like my paintings to hang in private homes but nowadays they tend to go to public collections.

Sunset Bonnet [1969]
Acrylic on canvas, 243.8 x 914.4 cm

The 30-foot canvas *Sunset Bonnet* was produced over the summer of the third year at the Royal College of Art and was part of an exhibition at the Royal Academy in 1969, organised by Carel Weight and Roger de Grey, 'Large Pictures for Public Places'. I cannot remember the source of it, but a very small advertisement would have impressed me enough to make a painting from it. It seemed mighty long, 30 feet, but it was not daunting.

It is based on a red car bonnet with light and clouds reflecting in it. I prepared the canvas with red paint and worked on top of that so the canvas became comparable to the surface of the car. This was something I had been building up to from the early days of working for Securicor and in the factories. It tickled me that I could use the bonnet as a carrying agent; everybody could relate to it and it led them into the painting without them being alienated by the thought that they were looking at something abstract.

There is a very formal structure to this painting, a set position for the cloud forms and the middle strut of the car bonnet; they all have their place and they all relate to one another. The central strut of the bonnet is at least a foot off the centre of the painting, which is important to me. To have it at the very central point of the canvas would have been too easy. I want the eye to travel around. To keep the onlooker involved, I had to play with a number of points on the canvas.

There is an illusion of space and depth. Once I had the light crimson base, I brought the luscious white creams and the darker reds in as needed. I would spray very heavily onto the canvas and, where shapes or edges were necessary, I would cut out bits of paper on the floor and fix them onto the canvas with masking tape and spray against them. In some respects it was a more immediate way of painting compared to my methods now. If the colour was too dark, I would spray white on it. Nowadays I colour mix, so it is a different procedure.

Size was important to me. This painting had to be consciously walked past: it was part of the environment.

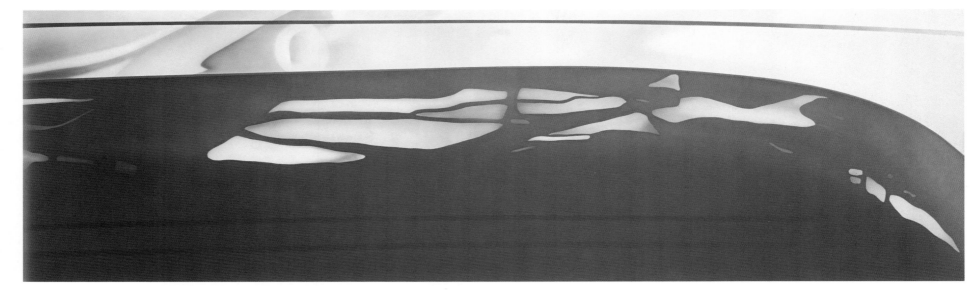

Green Fender [1969]
Acrylic on canvas, 121.9 x 365.8 cm

This is a classic painting with, perhaps, a Matisse or
Braque influence in the silhouettes of the shapes. It is
loosely based on the top of a car bonnet, which is a
very light green but has a side which is dark with an
interference of simple, light shapes that almost have
the feeling of birds floating across it.

The painting has some of the quality of a stained-
glass window. Every time I travel I go into churches.
The sort of light through a stained-glass window –
silhouetted, strong form – has always played a part in
my visual mentality. I feel easy with it.

Blue Base [1970]
Acrylic on canvas, 73.7 x 121.9 cm

In 1970 I worked on a series of smaller paintings, 29 inches by 48. I was using the rectangle and subdividing it. They were pushing my ideas and images a bit further. The screen and the markings on the bonnet were no longer as strong. They were less recognisably car parts and that was intentional.

Blue Highlight [1970]
Acrylic on canvas, 91.4 x 335.3 cm

This is a classic painting of this period. It uses a little bit of the structure, balance, light, flow and rhythm that later became important to me. Whilst it is recognisably a car bonnet with two ventilators (the dark shapes), I used the blackness or the emptiness of the space they created to make yet another shape or form on the canvas. In the middle of the reflection of the windscreen is the glow of the sun hitting the bonnet, so there is a division on one side balancing the other side. To break into the unity of the image with the glow of white was a development that came with this painting. The relationship between left and right is essential, yet the tonality and the wholeness of it is important, too. It is not simply a panel; it is a painting with a subject matter – however removed it is from that subject matter.

Blue Highlight took me four weeks' consistent work. I might have an idea stemming from a small reproduction about three inches by two inches and think "I can make something of this," but there comes a point, if I am making a 12-foot or a 15-foot painting, when it begins to have a life of its own. I am not interested in reproducing or re-creating. I am interested in the painting existing in its own right and having its own presence and life.

Around the time of *Blue Highlight* there was a painting that I worked on for about six months. I could not believe that I was unable to get it right and I worked and worked on it. It was a large painting, about 12 feet by 12 feet, and one evening I took it off the stretcher, screwed it up and put it in a large dustbin and jumped on it. I went to the pub and drank myself silly, came home and was horribly sick. I woke up early the next morning and I have never felt so good in my life. That yoke that was hanging round my neck was gone. That was a major failure. You have got to fail. It can be positive because from that failure you understand what was lacking. I must admit, I never worked out what was wrong with that painting. It should have worked, but it didn't. I probably needed more subject matter and content, something to relate to.

Reflector [1971]
Acrylic on canvas, 78.7 x 121.9 cm

Reflector exists both as a painting and as a print. It was a turning-point because it was the first time I used the environment – the building reflected in the bonnet – in the painting. It is strange how, as an artist, you can be blinkered for a long while. You can only take in so much at a time. Although I had been using surfaces that could reflect anything, up until now I had intentionally left out and chosen not to see all the reflected surfaces of the city in which I lived. I had not wanted to be tied to a specific environment and for a long time had wanted the paintings to be as general as possible, so that I could play with the marks and forms, the wiper blades, the ventilator shapes and so on. The change came when the subject matter became my own lookings and developments.

I realised when I did this painting that there were new elements coming in. Instead of the formulated areas of rhythms and movements of, for example, *Green Fender* (page 54),which were static, those of *Reflector* fanned out. There are indications of one or two new elements from the environment appearing, suggestions of what might come. But it was only hints in those days. I was just conscious of possibilities.

It is really important while you are working to keep looking, particularly in my case because the city and its apparatus is my environment. By this time I was going out regularly with a camera and sketchbook. I used a sketchbook until the chauffeur of one of the big, polished cars which was the subject of my sketching and who had been standing smoking, waited until I started drawing and then drove off laughing and waving. It was absolutely pointless trying to draw that quickly.

Reflector was also one of the few images in which I brought in a recognisable brand element, a detail from a Citroën headlight. I have always loved Citroëns – the headlight is sunk into the front wing of the car, a stunning piece of design – but it is unusual for me to make the detail recognisable because the cars are just the base from which the painting develops. I wanted the feel of the beautiful bend of the bonnet.

There is more illusion in this painting than in the flat surfaces I had been doing, a little bit of play within the headlamp area, which was rare for me. The decision to make the headlight so simple would have taken a lot of thought. I didn't want extraneous material to be brought in. Relatively speaking, the headlight encloses a great deal of activity in a small space, a tonal contrast and many divisions of light. I had to work hard to hold that activity and counterbalance it within the rest of the painting without making it look too busy.

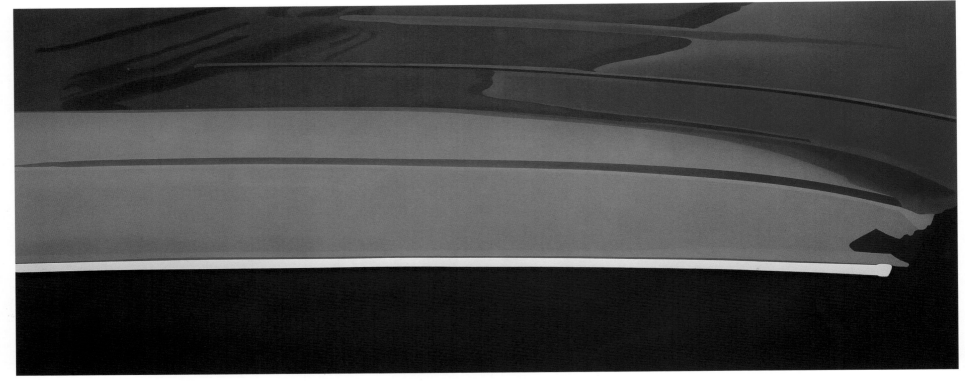

Blue Panel [1971]
Acrylic on canvas, 152.4 x 365.8 cm

This is a succulent painting. It is one of the few that I started and finished in a week and which I felt was highly successful. I had left the Royal College of Art by now, but I was still working 16-hour days in the studio. At this stage almost all the paintings were based on torn-out strips from magazines.

It is an image of the side of a car, but not as taut or tight as *Green Fender* (page 54). Because of the high sheen of the metal surface, my approach to texture was different in these years than it was later to become. By calling the paintings 'panel' and 'screen',

I was relating back to the Abstract Expressionists, who used the overall canvas even though they had divisions running along them. I use the word 'panel' to distinguish them from paintings with depth or space. These are very flat paintings with only a tiny bit of depth and, although the bonnets were the starting point, they were manipulated to make the painting succeed and the proportion is totally out of keeping with that of a car.

Today, my spaces are broken up and there are more structural areas within the canvases.

City Bonnet [1972]
Acrylic on canvas, 182.9 x 365.8 cm

This painting caused me enormous grief and hardship. I might even have destroyed it if it had not been for a student of mine, Richard Ballard, saying, "Brendan, that is the most important thing you have painted." Instead of destroying it, I carried on and it turned out to be a key work. It is the beginning of the break between car art, in its abstract sense, and reflected city art. It still uses the car and the break-up of the car body to cause the distortions of the reflections; these were part of my make-up by then. There was not a dramatic break – looking back I have not had any of those – but it does represent an important shift alongside other work of this time. Later, in 1973, I did *Mayfair I* and *II* (pages 62-63),

which took the idea even further forward.

City Bonnet definitely came from imagery I had collected walking round the City of London at the weekends and in the evenings. For a while, I had known exactly what I was doing; I had been using the publicity and posters and small reproductions in magazines as the basis of my paintings. Now I was trying to go further. No longer was the surface of the motor car providing me with enough; it had run its course. I loved having those paintings around me, but I needed more. Instead of playing with the idea of abstraction, I felt I had something to say about the environment and the city. The subject matter and its import had begun to change. The potential was increasing.

The Mayfair paintings

Mayfair I [1973-74]
Acrylic on canvas, 152.4 x 274.3 cm

The Mayfair paintings are a further development in my growing awareness of the environment, still using the car, but becoming more conscious of the buildings, their structures and windows. I had been going to Mayfair to make drawings and take photographs because that was the area to find a lot of grand, clean cars that reflected well.

These paintings are important because they were done just before I made the radical change of dropping the car as the information holder, and support structure, for the work. A number of paintings from this time remind me of Gaudi's architecture in Barcelona; they seem to be all over the place, with extreme pointed reflections, something I did not want. In contrast, the *Mayfair* paintings were fairly calm and static, and had a strong horizontal structure. I was very conscious of the play from top to bottom on the flat surface and I was beginning to have more confidence in dealing with architecture and city structures.

Mayfair II [1973-74]
Acrylic on canvas, 152.4 x 274.3 cm

City Sweep [1974]
Acrylic on canvas, 45.7 x 71.1 cm

City Sweep is a good title as this painting is almost sweeping out of control. I was becoming aware that I wanted more order and stability, but the work was ebbing and flowing all over the place. The car bonnet always distorted reflections in an extraordinary way and that was exactly what I was beginning not to need. I didn't want variation upon variation. The idea of using a different reflective point arose. That point became the building and, from that, a more solid and formal structure arrived. I didn't understand it in 1974, but when I did it was a sudden change. I moved to part-reflection and part-stasis, a quality of reality. It was a different drama.

Pimlico [1974]
Lithograph, 45.7 x 71.1 cm

It was this lithographic print that tipped me over. It just went too far. It troubled me in its extremity. I knew I had to change then and be more in control of what was happening. This is what interested me in Gaudi, just when he might stop.

I think he went too far.

This print seemed to have points everywhere. I used the reflection in a car body and all the houses, windows and everything else ended up in a flurry of points as the image developed. There was a structure there, but it didn't have the calmness I wanted. The actual reference points were becoming wilder and I didn't want to go down that path. The impetus was wrong from the beginning and didn't allow me to control or dictate or organise as I wanted to. The start is always crucial. Accident plays a part, but I can put myself in places where the ideas materialise, develop and then start.

The Manchester paintings

I was teaching one day a week in Manchester and I wanted to use local imagery.

I was struck by the strength of the buildings there. Like Birmingham, it is a city with heavy Victorian work with the grime of the 1940s and 1950s ingrained in it; I could relate to that even though I don't find it particularly attractive. At the time, areas of Manchester were being knocked down and removed and more human-related, contemporary buildings were going up. This site was part of a polytechnic or university and I would pass it every week or so and gradually my interest grew.

This series relates to *Pimlico* (page 65) where you get the extreme geometry. If I were to paint it now, I would do it differently. I like the bonnet and the way the slight cloud is gathering around a certain point, but I would not have the building as extreme and pointed as it appears here. I was gradually becoming aware that the distortion was getting out of hand and that the buildings themselves held an inherent attraction that, until then, I had not mined or manipulated. I believe it was from this building that the painting *Corner* (page 72) grew, a work that goes both back and forward and heralds the changes that took place from 1975-76.

Manchester I [1974]
Acrylic on paper, 47 x 69.8 cm

The Manchester paintings

Manchester II [1974]
Acrylic on paper, 47 x 69.8 cm

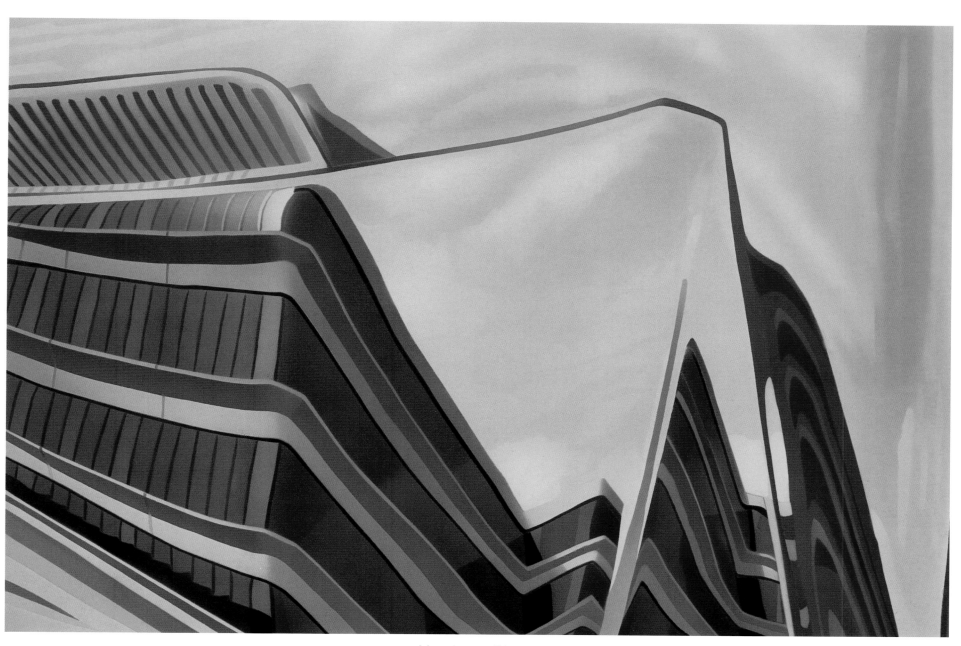

Manchester III [1974]
Acrylic on paper, 47 x 69.8 cm

City Windows [1974]
Acrylic on paper, 45.7 x 76.2 cm

This painting is arabesque. I enjoyed doing it but it didn't seem to be leading anywhere. It seems to be about design and pleasantries and shapes and forms without being hard-hitting and punchy in the way I would want it to be. The quality of decoration mitigated against what I wanted to achieve. I wanted something more functional and related to my environment. There is not much that is arabesque in a contemporary, tough city.

Pool Reflection [1975]
Acrylic on canvas, 137.2 x 213.3 cm

This is a total reflection in water. There is no stable element of the side of the pool or any other solid structure, it is utterly taken up with the rippling quality of the water. However, the painting has a layer or two – the sky is reflected through a window into the water, so I was dealing with several strata of reality. Some of the white areas were actually the backs of canvases reflected in the pool from the Basle Art Fair, which is where the idea for this began to germinate; I like the play of blank canvas on a canvas, but that was incidental. The distortion of the pool is nowhere near as extreme as the distortion of a car bonnet.

It is my first water painting and through its structure it relates to *Corner* (page 72). It was a natural progression from *Corner* to look at the more spread-out reflection in water, something I want to explore further in the future as I don't yet know how to use it. I enjoy looking at the Monets in Paris; I certainly don't want to paint like Monet, but I love the way he has treated water.

Corner [1975]
Acrylic on canvas, 137.2 x 213.3 cm

This was a turning-point, a very important painting. It moved me from total reflection to structured reflection. It is based roughly on a building I had used before in the car bonnets. I had made a number of images relating to this over a period of one or two years and, although they intrigued me, I could not think what to do with them. I was reviewing them in the studio and then, 'click', I had the idea and did it. Instead of having total distortion, what I wanted was the ability to have something concrete and solid on the canvas, against which to play all sorts of reflections and modulations.

The reflected building and the building which is reflecting meet at the corners, which makes it doubly striking. By placing that meeting point at the centre of the canvas I made it as powerful and immediate as it could be, and gained a simplicity and strength. Nowadays I will probably have many centre points.

By this time, the influence of Wesselmann and Rosenquist – in relation to scale, boldness and the choice of imagery culled from magazines and advertisements – had completely gone. Looking at *Corner* and *Manchester III* (page 69) together, a radical change has occurred within a year. *Corner* has a serene, dominant quality, whereas *Manchester* slips all over the place. The quietness and control of *Corner* were the qualities I was searching for. The strength and simplicity of the overall structure released a freedom to play.

Verandah [1976]
Acrylic on canvas, 137.2 x 213.3 cm

This is one of the few paintings where I had a break during the making of it. I had not finished it at the point when I went away to Cornwall for a family holiday, and when I came back I could not 'see' it. It was so delicate that it was difficult to perceive. That was a surprise because I had worked on it for three or four weeks, day and night. I had not noticed how subtle the drawing had become: I had to radically change that to bring the image back to existence.

I wanted something rippling but, in order to bring the underlying drawing back to life, I needed to be bolder and to strengthen the tones and hues. The drawn form of the veranda is, after all, described in paint within a small colour spectrum. The nature of my work directs that my palette is intentionally limited, which further increases the importance of tonal change.

The New York paintings

My first visit to New York was tremendously important, a voyage of discovery. I went for visual stimulus and it did not let me down at all. I was stunned to find one contemporary building after another. I went up to 57th Street and tried to walk all the way down logically, but it was not possible because there were interesting things on virtually every corner and I was side-tracked repeatedly. It fired me up.

I walked and looked and drew and, later, did a whole group of paintings stemming from the experience. I didn't want to use familiar landmarks like the Chrysler Building, I preferred to remain more abstract and anonymous. You are too tied to structure if the building is recognisable, and I like to be free to shift and add, take away and change as I choose. Anonymity means I can deal with the buildings in a purer manner and avoid decoration and flamboyancy.

The *New York* paintings are considerably freer than, for example, *Corner* (page 72), because by now I was able and willing to consider and include my feelings. In Manhattan I reacted to the space, the grandeur and the scale, and wanted to capture something of the city, whereas *Corner* was a simple, direct statement, exploiting a detail of the architecture simply as a starting point for a painting.

Building Projection comes from seeing one building totally reflected in another, the windows of one holding almost the whole of the other. Because they were so close together I could not see them in their entirety unless I gazed up. I wanted to capture the height and the sheer proximity of them both.

The verticals are critically important. They are strong and dominate the painting, sweeping from bottom to top, and they are held in place by the small window-pane structures. I find the repetition of the hundreds of windows that you get in New York bedazzling and enjoyable, and I can use that repetition and variation like musical notation. I remember playing with the pane structures in *Building Projection*, so that there is a swing from diagonal left to right moving across the canvas. I wanted to bring the viewer slap bang against the building to give the sensation of being immersed in the painting as if it were an environment.

City Reflection is the nearest I get to a New York street scene as opposed to a single building, but it is still quite abstracted. It was stimulated by a building which curves inwards. Half the canvas is bathed in light and the other half is quite dark. I like the vast, empty area with the complexity and darkness almost framing it. Within the white there is a lot of subtlety, and in the dark areas I use abstract shapes like hieroglyphics or writing to form beautiful rhythms, moves and breaks. The shapes interrupt the darkness as if to show the viewer a way inside, and they also imply activity. One of the main features about my work is the lack of drawn human figures but within the abstracted marks I am able to get the feeling of bustle and noise.

The New York paintings

Building Plane [1977]
Acrylic on canvas, 138.4 x 208.3 cm

Building Projection [1977]
Acrylic on canvas, 208.3 x 138.4 cm

The New York paintings

City Reflection [1977]
Acrylic on canvas, 138.4 x 208.3 cm

Seven Columns [1978]
Acrylic on canvas, 208.3 x 138.4 cm

The New York paintings

Whilst I was in New York I never once went into a gallery because there was so much richness in the street, and I could not tear myself away, in case I missed something. This painting luxuriates in the sheer power of that environment and celebrates the mass of window panes by allowing them to rush up the canvas. There is a great strength to the surface, formed by the panes in their angular procession across the canvas, as well as in the vertical surge, and that hardness, in turn, relates back to the car panels. The subtlety of the grey blues and hints of green is offset by two columns of intense blue, whilst the depth comes only through the reflections.

Exterior [1978]
Acrylic on canvas, 208.3 x 138.4 cm

Awning [1979]
Acrylic on canvas, 142 x 238 cm

With this I got as close to a shaped canvas as I could without literally shaping it. The structure is as strong as I am ever likely to use. It is one of the few paintings where reflections play a secondary part and are almost incidental. It is a sleek, strange painting and I am never sure whether I like it or not.

Victoria Street [1981]
Acrylic on canvas, 76.2 x 76.2 cm

Although this is a busy area of London near a main-line railway terminus and a large coach station, it can be strangely impersonal. It is, of course, a place of transience. Bill Mallabar, who ran a graphics agency and with whom I worked on a number of commissions, had arranged that I produce a series of paintings for Elemeta, the firm which provided the glass for many contemporary buildings, one of which is in Victoria Street. I went back to look hard at the site and to try to respond to the flux and movement as well as the architecture. I used the regimentation of the structure to contrast with the ebb and flow of the reflections, and there is an almost castle-like solidity to the form on the canvas; Westminster Cathedral is close behind and, though not formally in the painting, it certainly existed there in my mind.

Tolmer Square [1981]
Acrylic on canvas, 78.7 x 99.1 cm

Tolmer Square is a landmark at the end of Tottenham Court Road. At night – the only time that the traffic abates and when peace settles around it – the building reminds me of a huge ship, steadfast and glowing powerfully, in the middle of the city. The flux and change that constantly surround it seem to affect the fabric of the building itself and it was this that captured my imagination. The upright window supports are straining and pulling against the overall rigidity. I wanted to include the sky sections to add stability and the suggestion of space.

By my second and third visits to New York I was able to get beyond the grandeur and bombast and begin discovering quieter areas. This one was near Wall Street, not such a contemporary part, architecturally. The painting is about my reactions to and reflections on New York without being so tied to its modernity. It is an image to do with seeing through and beyond, breaking into; a little like pulling the curtain back and going beneath the surface.

Cross Grid [1981]
Acrylic on canvas, 86.4 x 76.2 cm

Cumbrian landscapes

I was invited to participate in an exhibition about Cumbrian landscapes, 'Presences of Nature'. It was expected that I would paint the nuclear power station at Windscale. I went to Cumbria with my wife and daughters and we went to Windscale, which I knew straightaway I had no desire to paint, and we looked in Keswick and various towns for an alternative subject.

I realised that the strength of the landscape itself would give me a structure and, although it initially seemed different, there were similarities between it and the city structures I felt in tune with. I don't think of clouds as wispy things being blown about; I tend to see them as citadels or akin to buildings. The Cumberland skies were stunning and what I saw there in a few days fed me for some time to come. It was October so, from a painter's point of view, we had the best of weather; it alternated between rumbling dark daylight, sleet, rain and snow, with beautiful blue breaking through occasionally. One of my clearest memories is of being on top of a mountain and the phenomenal strength of the black clouds as they rolled towards us.

I did three paintings and it was the first time since my college days that I worked from the natural landscape. Clouds had already begun to play a part in my city buildings, but I found the Cumbrian clouds so rich and full that they could occupy almost the total canvas. I was lucky to be invited to be part of 'Presences of Nature' because it extended my vision and the possibilities I could use; I discovered that I was not walled within the town and could shift freely wherever I wanted. I went on to paint in Dartmoor and through that, began to realise not only how different parts of Britain are one from another, but how differently the weather behaves in, say, Scotland, London, Dartmoor and the Lake District.

Cumbrian landscapes

Cumbrian Landscape I [1981-82]
Acrylic on canvas, 88.9 x 129.5 cm

Cumbrian Landscape II [1981-82]
Acrylic on canvas, 88.9 x 129.5 cm

I am not interested in painting a portrait of a building. Often when you look into a building, it will seem to move or it will appear that the lines of it are not straight or parallel. It is this kind of aspect that intrigues me and I can increase the impact of that because of the way I work. In this case, I used the ploy of sub-dividing the canvas with a strong diagonal line, part way down on the right and left-hand sides and between these I have placed what I consider the important elements of The Economist building. The diagonal lines which occupy a space in the sky, and drive through the painting may have been something – perhaps the lighting or flooring – in the building holding the reflection of The Economist building; I would have decided to incorporate them more fully in the painting to seduce the eye.

I have also altered the windows slightly. It was the beginning of using little incidents, light and dark, to break up the glass area itself just using simple lines and simple tonal and colour changes.

The Economist Building [1983]
Acrylic on canvas, 162.6 x 147.3 cm

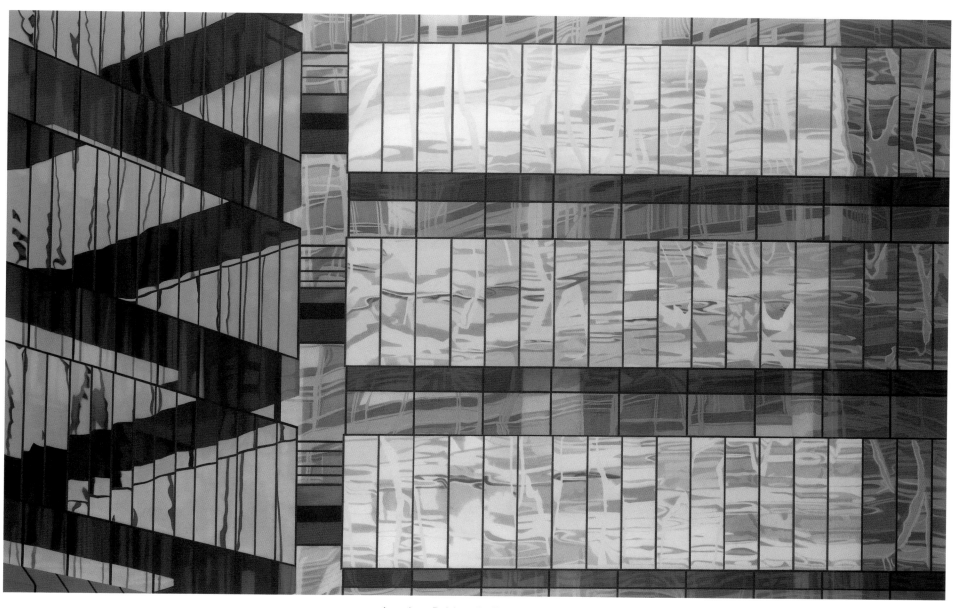

London Bridge Reflection [1984]
Acrylic on canvas, 147.3 x 228.6 cm

Guys Hospital, the railway station and the offices
poised above it bring a constantly moving population
to this part of London. The left section of my painting
related to the railway tracks and the noise of the
carriages crossing the sleepers, feeding in a suggestion
of space and order. This contrasts with the surface
activity on the right. It is an absorbing place, fluid
and changing.

This new building replaced the old fish market. The number of grids and their angles interested me. It is a painting of structural simplicity but with many facets. I was able to incorporate not only the sky, but the sky and reflected struts and also reflections of the reflections – but all held in place by three simple structures. I like looking at this one.

Billingsgate [1985]
Acrylic on canvas, 213.3 x 121.9 cm

Pontiac [1986]
Acrylic on canvas, 91.4 x 139.7 cm

This painting was a commission relating to a television advertisement for Gillette in which they used a Pontiac. I was asked if I could do a painting which they could use for static advertising. I liked the idea of that and also of having the Gillette lettering reflected in the car. What I didn't want was a silhouette of the car. I didn't know how to use the extremities of the canvas around the car, so I brought in texture and allowed it to play within the fender as well as in the surround. Twenty years later I was to re-use the idea of texture in the *Dubrovnik* (pages 146-151) and *Dubai* (pages 144 and 152) paintings.

Fifteen years prior to painting *Pontiac*, the headlight alone had been the subject matter of *Reflector* (page 58) and this canvas contains many of the same elements. In this case I was intent on making it recognisably a Pontiac and all that meant – Americanisms, extremes, drive-in cinemas, gum-chewing, guzzling youth, confidence. It is big, bold and brassy.

This is a small painting. It is based on something I saw in Times Square in New York. I liked the idea of including lettering which said something but which was not quite legible. If you read this painting in a mirror, you could see that it says Gordon's, but that is not the important point and, similarly, if the writing was easily readable it would disturb the overall image.

It took ages to get the computer dot effect. I got a needle and made all the dots in a bit of paper and then sprayed through that. I often say to students that if they are going to be an artist, they must learn to do things absolutely and to take things to an extreme, until the methods work as they want them to. Although all the little dots in this painting don't play an overtly big part they are terribly important and, added together, make it a better painting.

The crimson, yellow, blue and orange of *Gordon's* are unusual colours for me. I look on this as a very jolly, light and bright little painting and it was a pleasure to do.

Gordon's [1986]
Acrylic on paper, 21 x 18 cm

Terminal 4 [1986]
Acrylic on canvas, 243.8 x 121.9 cm each

I was invited to Terminal 4 at Heathrow Airport to meet the architect, the designer and the art adviser. The proposal was that my paintings should be positioned immediately opposite the passport control gate, in the pre-boarding lounge. From the outset I realised the major problem would be scale and, although each one of the quartet of paintings is eight feet tall and four feet wide, they were small against the massive scale of the building. For the time they remained in the building they attracted positive attention, but the Airport Authority redesigned the area in order to make it clearer to passengers which way they needed to go for their flights and the paintings were moved to the boardroom.

The paintings were based upon the exterior of the building, the idea being to bring the outside inside. Elements of colour and structure take the eye across the broad spread but the subject matter of each painting is different and they remain independent. They are hung with an inch of space between them and, although it was important to regard them as a set, I realised the four didn't need to be of equal dominance, and allowed two to act in a supportive role.

The Lloyd's paintings

Lloyd's – The Stairwell [1986-87]
Acrylic on paper, 21 x 18 cm

One Sunday morning I was walking in the City with my daughter Lucy, and I looked up and saw all these tubes being reflected and I knew immediately I would have to paint them. I had no choice, it was such an extraordinary sight. It is rare that something zaps me immediately, usually finding a subject for a painting is a long process of trawling, standing, waiting, drawing and photographing. What I was looking at was Richard Rogers' new Lloyd's building reflected in a tiny window in one of the small roads leading up to it. It had caused controversy as it was one of the first buildings that had all its innards on the outside – all the pipes and tubes and services were quite visible and it had intriguing lifts going up the outside of the structure. There was talk about it looking like a laundry with all its washing hanging out in full view.

From my point of view it was a group of aluminium tubes resting upon one another, and that related right back to Léger; whether he was painting sailors, builders or females lying across couches, Léger's work always had the same robust feel. Lloyd's inspired me to do a series of eight paintings over approximately two years, some large, some small, looking at it from different angles. I loved using the circular forms and being able to revel in them. It was so intriguing I just wanted to paint it more and more.

Unlike Léger, I was not using the tubular forms as anything other than parts of the building, but for the first time I became aware of how sculptural a building can be. With this series I could concentrate on rotund forms rather than dealing with fleeting, reflected images. I wanted to bring out the sheer joy and physicality of the tubes and cylinders in contrast to the evenness and repetition of so many other modern designs. I remember revelling in the pleasure of being able to work almost three-dimensionally on a two-dimensional surface, and to make elements move from light to dark to light in order to give them body.

The building occupies a very small land space and is tucked into its plot and is not easily viewed from any single point so, probably, reflections in other buildings are the best way of looking at it. In a strange way, Lloyd's is a very light building and almost springs from the ground so that you feel it must be held down otherwise it might float away. I wanted to contrast that quality with the formal heaviness of elements such as the diagonal supports that I used in the paintings; I, too, needed formal elements to tie the image down. Maybe I was trying to imprison the building, prevent it from running away.

The Lloyd's paintings

Lloyd's [1986-87]
Acrylic on canvas, 228.6 x 147.3 cm

Lloyd's – The Tubes [1987]
Acrylic on paper, 20.3 x 17.8 cm

Alfa Romeo [1988]
Acrylic on canvas, 90 x 122 cm

A friend owns 20 Alfa Romeos and he once hurtled me round a race-track in three horrid laps, during which time I breathed only once. Despite this, it was totally seductive to work in his garage and see the moulded shapes, each one so distinctive from the rest.

The machines took me back to my early painting days and I was happy to relate to the geometry of the car bodies, and in *Alfa Romeo* and *White Curve and Lattice*, I wanted to show my great pleasure in the stimulus of these beautifully sculptured beasts.

White Curve and Lattice [1988]
Acrylic on canvas, 53.3 x 61 cm

Kembrey Park [1989]
Acrylic on canvas, 76 x 101 cm

Kembrey Park was my first commission for Aukett
Associates, the firm of architects. I enjoyed the
environment they had created and it triggered many
ideas. Gradually this painting emerged, a response to
the expansive quality and complexity of the place.
Although it is quite a small canvas, the broad sweep of
the railings creates a feeling of space.

Kembrey Trellis [1989]
Acrylic on canvas, 76 x 101 cm

This painting followed on from *Kembrey Park* and was again based upon the site designed by Aukett. The fascination remained with this space and its openness. I felt free and easy and encouraged to walk around. The tubular structures form arches through which to stroll. I have simplified everything to dramatise the power and presence of the tubes.

Dartmoor Skyscape Across Gidleigh Common [1989]
Acrylic on canvas, 129.5 x 182.9 cm

Remote places like Dartmoor have a tremendous aura, a spirit and power that attracts me greatly. Going to remote places is a harking back to childhood when I lived at Lowestoft, the most easterly point of Great Britain. In Dartmoor I remember feeling as if we were enclosed and that the sky was a ceiling attracted to the earth. It was a terrific sensation. Even the noise of the nearby traffic could not deflect the sense of history and of the previous generations who belonged in that place.

The sky in this painting is very structured and, to some degree, held in place by land running parallel to the bottom of the canvas. Among the interesting features of the area are the ancient standing stones and the odd shapes they make against the horizon; I used just a bit of one – silhouetted against the light – to tie the painting down.

London Bridge [1989]
Acrylic on canvas, 162.6 x 233.7 cm

After so many paintings of the particular, this one gives a general feel of the city I live in, London. It captures the spaciousness and the peculiar towers from the churches. The abstract element is important yet it does not destroy the figurative effect.

The InterCity paintings

I had no inkling that I would be working from train stations even though I had always loved train travel. As a child I was allowed to pull the whistle on steam trains and to ride in the cab, and I remember porters from the days of the Orient Express, and the sense of exotic travel and overnight journeys. Coming out of the station in Rome is another vivid memory.

I was offered the opportunity to paint British stations by the architect, Jane Priestman, whom I had met when I worked on the *Terminal 4* painting (page 93). I was given a retainer to look at all the stations and then reported back to InterCity. It was decided that the paintings should celebrate the electrification of the East coast and the new 225 train, and this meant basing my work on the route between Kings Cross and Edinburgh.

Over the next months, I paced the stations, always passing through Kings Cross, which, inevitably, proved the hardest image to win. The key stations were Kings Cross, York, Leeds, Newcastle and Edinburgh, and it was a stunning commission because it took me travelling with the purpose of being in each station until I could take back its essence to my studio and work with it. There were sparkling possibilities, such as the mixture of the new and the old within Newcastle station. The only difficult environment was Leeds, which was dark, and in which I opted to use an engine incorporating some of the colour of the city brick to link it to the locality. York has a splendid Victorian roof – it reminded me of a cathedral – and I decided to contrast that with the technology that carried the electrification; the pinpoints of light in the metal were like church windows and I made them intentionally uneven and distorted. In at least two of the paintings – *Edinburgh* and *Newcastle* – I wanted the rhythm of the structures to suggest the noise of the wheels on the track and its repetitive quality.

In each of the paintings I included the InterCity emblem, the swallow symbol and took care that it should not be too dominant – sometimes I have to search for it myself. The paintings were hung in the boardroom of Euston House, but they were commissioned to be used as the basis for posters on the station platforms, an idea I wholly supported.

London Kings Cross [1990]
Acrylic on canvas, 91.4 x 58.4 cm

The InterCity paintings

York [1990]
Acrylic on canvas, 91.4 x 58.4 cm

Leeds [1990]
Acrylic on canvas, 91.4 x 58.4 cm

The InterCity paintings

Newcastle [1990]
Acrylic on canvas, 91.4 x 58.4 cm

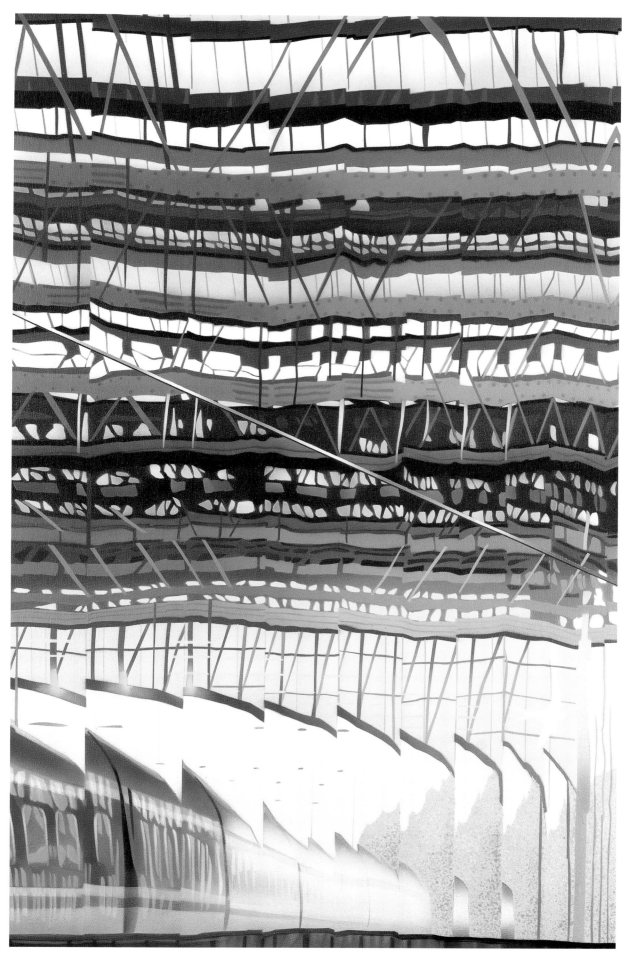

Edinburgh [1990]
Acrylic on canvas, 91.4 x 58.4 cm

The InterCity paintings

Carriage Window [1990]
Acrylic on canvas, 91.4 x 58.4 cm

This came as a result of the InterCity series and it was the first time I had left one of the stations while working on the commission. I spent days wandering around Bath thinking and looking. It is like a stage-set. After the Crescent, the Baths and the resplendent buildings, I felt I wanted to include the bridge and the water running through the city. In the water I was able to capture the solidity and grandeur of the period building and I combined this – in the top corner – with the suggestion of the slight turbulence of the flow as it tipped over the fall. The circular arch of the bridge introduces a sense of timelessness and space, and the feeling of going beyond into something different. As with the other InterCity images, this one was made into a poster and has proved extremely popular.

Bath [1992]
Acrylic on canvas, 91.4 x 58.4 cm

This relates to *Pontiac* (page 91). The dots used here were not so much for texture but more to break up the surface and to vary the hue. The title is important and I chose it because it seemed a quiet, poetic and pretty painting. After all the dominant, ebullient work that preceded it, I needed a break; it was like hearing a beautiful piece of music, perhaps Jacqueline du Pré playing Elgar's cello concerto.

Murmurs [1990]
Acrylic on canvas, 76.2 x 58.4 cm

Gathering Clouds [1991]
Acrylic on canvas, 162.6 x 233.7 cm

I like the drama of this painting. It is partly derived
from something I saw and partly invention.

Cloudscapes

Cloudscape I [1991]
Acrylic on canvas, 50.8 x 76.2 cm

These were based upon my experience in Dartmoor. They are pure cloudscapes with no tie to the land. There were always going to be four varying aspects of robust clouds, different structures rather than at different times of the day. It was pure pleasure to paint these and I did them as an unbroken quartet, where the tightness of one would relax me into the next. In *Cloudscape IV*, one cloud grows from another, which I like tremendously. I would like to do a series of skies that relate to the seasons and changes of light, and perhaps these are heading towards that.

Cloudscape II [1991]
Acrylic on canvas, 50.8 x 76.2 cm

Cloudscape III [1991]
Acrylic on canvas, 50.8 x 76.2 cm

Cloudscape IV [1991]
Acrylic on canvas, 50.8 x 76.2 cm

Cumulus [1991]
Silkscreen, edition of 60, 152.4 x 121.9 cm
Diploma Work, Royal Academy of Arts

Cumulus is the largest print I have ever done and it was the one I gave to the Royal Academy of Arts when I was elected in 1992. It is a complex image that works on various visual levels; you see one structure and then another structure, the windows, and then within the windows there is yet another structure. Underpinning it all are the clouds. The experience of working out in the natural landscape has given me confidence to work with skies and clouds.

I have brought the cloud into this print as directly, fully and richly as possible even though the image is very much to do with the city and its grids and structures. I liked the idea of counterpointing the two elements and giving a softness to something that was hard-edged. Even though the image has straight lines, you get the whispering forms; the harshness and hardness are almost camouflaged. At the very bottom is a little tube, a happy remembrance of the Lloyd's tubes and an echo of Léger.

Turbulence [1992]
Acrylic on canvas, 91 x 121.5 cm

Turbulence had the elements I wanted in a painting at the time I did it, just enough building, but not too much.

It is probably my most Turneresque painting. I love Turner. He showed how abstract you could be whilst still being a figurative artist. His treatment of mist and sky and water and weather is outstanding. He is really a contemporary artist. I was so intrigued with it that I worked on a smaller version as well, although I never saw the two together and probably never will now, as one has gone to Sicily.

The clouds dominate the painting but behind them is a girder, which is partially hidden by them. I liked the interplay between something so man-made and so basic to the 20th century and the eternal element of the clouds. I find this more mysterious than most of my paintings, almost romantic. It has more to do with feeling and idea, than with vision and form.

One of the great pleasures of being commissioned is in the travelling and exploring of various parts of the country. This commission from Aukett took me to the countryside close to Horsham. The building stands very powerfully in the landscape and yet, strangely, as contemporary as it is, it fits in very well.

Lennox Wood [1992]
Acrylic on canvas, 30 x 39 cm

To have the sunset at the base moving though green to the sky blue at the top seemed quite appropriate, for there is a terrific panorama from the steps. The vastness was expressed through cloud and colour, broken into by the metal supports. I really liked the intrusion of the bolts grouped within the image.

Toltec Sunset [1992]
Silkscreen print, 76 x 50 cm

Riverside [1993]
Acrylic on canvas, 175.3 x 121.9 cm

Riverside is based upon an early morning walk beside the River Thames, on a beautiful spring morning, absolutely fresh. I had been along this Embankment several times before and been intrigued; on this inspirational day I understood what I might be able to do. I passed a window looking into a very tall room, bare, except for a plant. It gave me the idea of trying to do a painting which had the elements of a country landscape along with some of the structures and strictures of the town. Within it, I wanted to get the feel of being by the river without necessarily having the elements of the river in it; I wanted to capture that fluidity.

This was quite a different painting half-way through. I began with the thin, light grey cruciform at a diagonal across the front of the painting. Although the cruciform is the hardest area, it sinks into the painting and does not dominate because of the lightness of its tone; it is an enigma. The metal beams (which supported the building) would have been drawn in very early on and very solidly. It was not the painting I wanted – this is where one is not totally in control – so, although I put them in strong, perhaps I knew they would be camouflaged or disappear.

The structure established, then came the plant and the clouds, and with them, the enjoyment and the pleasure. This was the first time I brought vegetation into the studio. It was important that the leaves had a reality in themselves, however abstracted they became. I wanted the feel of the huge sky and to have a softness going from the bottom right through to the top, breaking into the hard structure of the building. I used the fleeting, fleece cloud to help achieve this and to give a suggestion of movement across the canvas. Even the shadows of the leaves allowed me to soften the edges, a further breakdown of the metallic, man-made structure.

I remember this painting as being optimistic and enjoyable. When you are working, you don't think of the troubles of the last painting, you deal with the present. It goes back to my having begun to train as a priest; when you are hearing confession, you exclude other thoughts. I worried about the relative strength of the beams and it fascinates me that in the end there is so little of them. Yet the viewer is aware of them being there, which is exactly what I wanted.

Freeflow is a partner to *Riverside* (page 120) and was determined by the clouds falling into the huge blue atrium. The cloud is much more contained in this one, which also has much more definite contrasts than the softer *Riverside*.

Freeflow [1993]
Acrylic on canvas, 175.3 x 121.9 cm

This was done to celebrate the 40th birthday of a good friend, Melanie. It is a musical painting – the intense blue of the three middle struts relates to jazz, with a ripple and movement either side – hence the title.

Meli's Blues [1993]
Acrylic on canvas, 26 x 20 cm

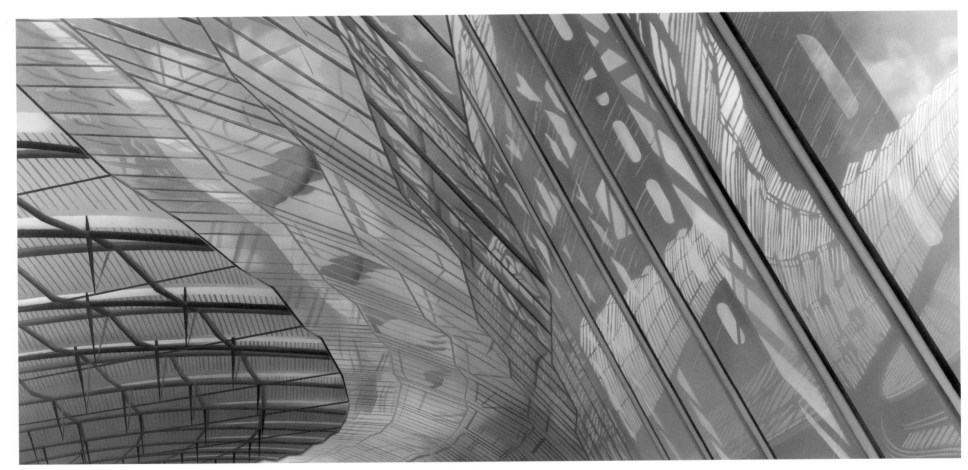

Waterloo International [1993]
Acrylic on canvas, 152.5 x 304.8 cm

The architect Nicholas Grimshaw was given a brief to create a covering for the new platforms for the London-Paris Channel Tunnel trains. He had to accept the existing station at Waterloo and what he has built is one of the most stunning modern environments I have been in. The whole beauty of it is not so much downstairs, which is pretty good, but upstairs with the snake-like glass over the station, and the way it curves and gets thinner and thinner, and then expands again. You see reflections and light and the scudding clouds, the London buildings and a distant view of the River Thames. It is regrettable that when you catch a train to Paris you are not called to the platform until the train is ready and soon to move out, so you have only a few minutes to appreciate it all.

I had seen the site virtually before the terminus was started, certainly I was there when the blue struts were put into place on giant cranes and the glass was put in. I had grown up with the building as I worked on ideas for the painting; it was quite some time before any trains or human beings inhabited it. Since the tunnel is glass, it was quite different being there in good light, bad light, night light. When it rained, the noise on the panes and the way the water rippled down the windows was incredible.

It was totally up to me how I wanted to use the site. I thought of doing a whole-length view, including the little whiteness of the exit but I decided against that. I decided it must be a long painting so as to give the sense of extension. I chose a cross-view to get the feeling of the curve, which is a crucial aspect of the building itself. The drawings took ages and ages and there are lots of details that I didn't put in because they became too fussy and it is not a fussy building. The final work evolved from an accumulation of drawings and photographs, an amalgam of perspectives. In reality, it would have been impossible to get all the reflections at once.

Three-quarters of the structure is glass but there is also aluminium as well as the very bright blue supports. I wanted the feeling of inside and outside, and of travel. Although it is not very obvious, what I actually did was use the reflection of the tracks to give the feeling of the motion of the train, and the regular noise you get from that. I then used sections of the large metal supports that run up the outside of the building to break into the tracks so that I achieved a kind of irregular regularity, again enhancing the feeling of motion. Although there are no people in the painting, I wanted the implication of busyness and activity and this I did not only through all the little shifts in the reflections of the tracks, but also the way the light filtered through some of the metal supports.

I had sample pieces of the struts in my studio and without them I might not have believed they were so blue.

Waterloo International is a remembrance of the opening of the building, but for me it went further and describes the beginning of a journey and the adventure; I look at it and think of the excitement ahead when you have been through customs at Waterloo and are on your way to Paris and the snails and great wines.

Brighton Pavilion [1993]
Acrylic on canvas, 81.3 x 121.9 cm

I was made Professor of Painting at Brighton University in 1996 and have taught there for many years so, when the University commissioned this painting as part of a touring show that began at The Redfern Gallery, I knew the quality of the image that I wanted although I was not sure how it should be determined. I considered the Pier and the Regency terraces and then thought of the Pavilion and, after looking at it a great deal, decided that it contained the elements that could describe Brighton for me.

One aspect that has always fascinated me is the startling summer light there and I was able to illustrate this in the cream whiteness of the Pavilion stone – so concentrated that it almost hurts the eyes – and the intense blue of the water. I wanted my painting to shimmer on the canvas and, although the Pavilion is not on the seafront, I found a muddy puddle in the grounds, and made use of that to reflect the building.

My brother Bryan and I had discussed the possibility of a painting from Reading College where he worked. He loved the idea of the various uses it could be put to. After some lovely lunches and tours around the campus I took my imagery back to the studio and started work. It was not too easy at first but the picture grew and developed. I had to use the brick and wood, these were basic to the building. But I wanted to create space and this was achieved by cloud floating behind the front structure. The solidity of the wooden bars and the tactile quality of the brick contrast beautifully with the softness of the rest of the painting – it is as though these provide the gateway through into the painting.

Reading College [1993]
Acrylic on canvas, 76.2 x 50.7 cm

Passing Cloud [1994]
Acrylic on paper, 22.9 cm diam.

Storm Cloud [1994]
Acrylic on paper, 22.9 cm diam.

The Head of the Royal Academy Enterprises invited
me to produce some images that could be used on a
plate and a mug. I decided to develop a set of five
images that I was interested in at the time and from
which the RA could choose the most suitable.

I had always wanted to work within a circle. Was it
possible to have no top, no bottom and no edge? In
my case, the answer was, "not really". The image for
the mug was continuous, whereas *Storm Cloud* has the
dark and light divided by a silver lining, and, above
this, the contrast of light whispy clouds suggesting
wind and change.

This painting is based on Glasgow Central Station, which has a lot of great qualities that go unnoticed at the level of the human eye. You have got to look up and around, which is precisely what I did for this painting.

Central [1994]
Acrylic on canvas, 91.4 x 58.4 cm

I was given a free hand within this painting to decide the colour and logo for Great Western, who had not yet been given the franchise for the trains.

I had not worked from Paddington before, although I had been there often, and it was a great pleasure to incorporate Brunel's magnificent station within my work.

Great Western at Paddington [1994]
Acrylic on canvas, 101.6 x 63.5 cm

The ScotRail paintings

Scotrail commissioned me to work on what became six 'destination' paintings, five of which were of the Western Highlands. These were the basis for the posters now being used on their stations, and I was conscious when I was making the paintings that they would have to work in that format, and to make people aware of the possibilities of travel.

It was wonderful to have lots of trips to the Western Highlands because I had learnt about the history of the region at school. You can go through terrible rain and snowstorms in that part of the world and then the day can change radically, and provide an idea for an image. That happened with *Loch Shiel* when my wife, Hilary, and I were in Glenfinnan. We saw the most stunning sunset and I realised it was what I would do, both as a painting and a print. The painting is more refined than the print, with more subtlety in the sky and softer edges to the cloud – with a painting, the ability to make the image subtle is literally at my fingertips, whereas the printmaking process is more complicated and removed. There are several other differences between the painting and the print, the most apparent being that a statue commemorating Bonnie Prince Charlie appears in the painting, a detail that could not be made to work on the print so I took him out entirely.

The partner to *Loch Shiel* is *Glencoe*. It is a tougher, colder, more abstract image whereas *Loch Shiel* is romantic and more traditional. Again, the idea for *Glencoe* occurred on a day of heavy rain and mist, when the downpour stopped abruptly and suddenly there were clouds scudding across a blue sky. Although it was not on the list of places that I had been commissioned to do, I had no doubt I would paint it for all its qualities of mystery and illusion. It is a place steeped in history and I go back there now every time I visit Scotland whether it is snowing, raining or brilliant sunshine. The road at Glencoe runs between two high sets of mountains and, rather than doing the valley with mountains on either side, I was able to get the feeling of enclosure and tightness using the mountain reflected in the water.

Not all the ScotRail series were landscapes. For example, *Glenmorangie Still* is based on a distillery in Tain. I spent many hours there, drawing, photographing and looking, and was given a tour during which all the processes were explained to me. Some rooms were romantic, for instance the sight of cask after cask going into the distance, but I felt the atmosphere in that one was rather gloomy.

Later, I went back to the distillery alone and spent a lot of time in the room with the containers, each of which holds about 11,000 litres of whisky. I wandered around and touched the containers, lay down, stood up, just getting to know the room as fully as possible. It was an unusual environment, weird and other-worldly. (Although the company is the biggest producer of malt whisky in the world, the total workforce is about 15 men. I was there for long periods alone and occasionally someone would come to the console, press a button and disappear.) I could never spend more than four hours at a time in there because the smell grew too heavy.

Gradually, ideas arose about how I might work using the containers and these intimations were developed in my studio. Even though they have been in use for years, the containers are amazing, futuristic looking objects. They are made of copper, so there is tremendous sheen and shine and, as they are rounded, there is no end of abstract reflections. I chose to work from a section of one of the containers and wanted to achieve an abstract image capable of conveying the flavour, taste and smell of whisky through the flow and transparency of the paint quality. I had made a few colour notes on site, but I didn't do much drawing there as the shape was so simple and regular.

The canvas for this one was a bright orange, which is unusual for me. I laid down six oranges, not absolutely pure, but burnt Sienna and with other colours mixed in for richness. There needed to be a shimmer and a depth; I wanted a huge glow, something as amber looking as possible, with the quality that you get from a highly polished surface.

The ScotRail paintings

Loch Shiel [1995]
Acrylic on canvas, 101.6 x 63.5 cm

Glencoe [1995]
Acrylic on canvas, 101.6 x 63.5 cm

The ScotRail paintings

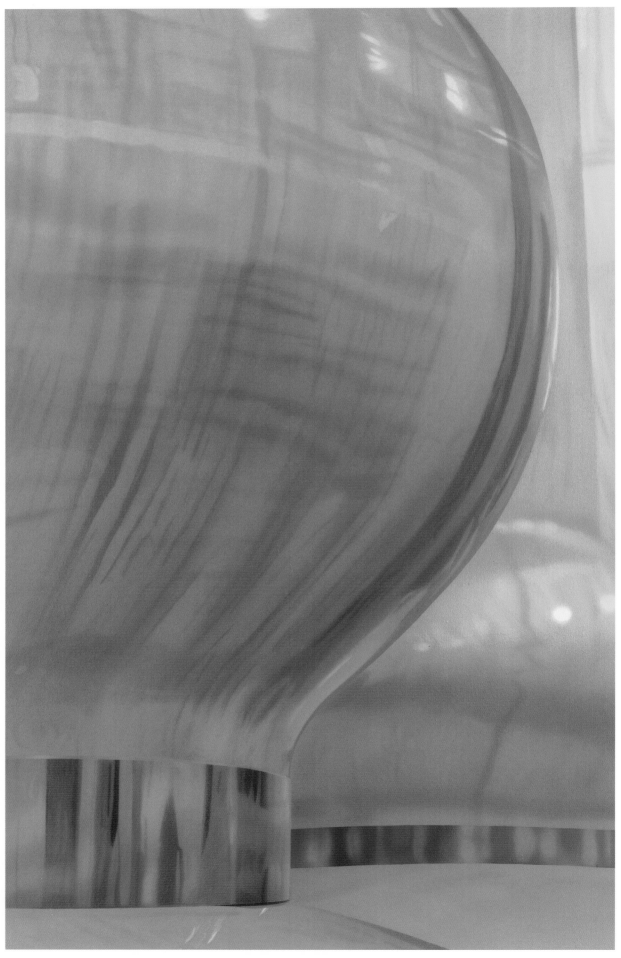

Glenmorangie Still [1995]
Acrylic on canvas, 101.6 x 63.5 cm

Quiraing, Isle of Skye [1995]
Acrylic on canvas, 101.6 x 63.5 cm

The ScotRail paintings

Glenfinnan [1995]
Acrylic on canvas, 101.6 x 63.5 cm

Nevis Range [1996]
Acrylic on canvas, 101.6 x 63.5 cm

This was a commission from the Community College in Hackney which, like all colleges, is competing for students, and needed to raise its profile and establish itself visually as well as in a written manner. The brief was to base the painting on the locality of the College. Right opposite the College is a beautiful, classic church, within the sound of Bow Bells, and part of the history and heritage of that part of London. I felt that, in appealing to scholars all over the world, the painting should include the new as well as the old and, by good luck, Waterloo International (the Channel Tunnel terminus) is also nearby; you could not get much newer than that! The image is based on those two buildings and I have also assimilated the emblem of the College – the purply rectangle at the top – which I put in early on so that it would not stick out too much.

Shoreditch Church and Waterloo International [1995]
Acrylic on canvas, 101.6 x 63.5 cm

The Gatwick Express paintings

Eros Piccadilly [1996]
Acrylic on canvas, 101.6 x 63.5 cm

These paintings were commissioned by Gatwick Express, who wanted images to suggest the heart of London.

The painting of Eros in Piccadilly Circus relates to *Gordon's* (page 92), the image based on Times Square. The lettering is more recognisable here but because of the reflective way I have used it, it is no more important than the overall design. I enjoyed painting the lettering in reverse because it meant I could treat it as a rich and powerful abstract statement, and all the whites and yellows and darks work nicely round the statue of Eros itself. The statue took me ages to draw because I had to remember the body and all its muscles; it made me realise how grateful I am for the life drawing I did at the Royal College of Art in my student days. The wings were a different problem – I had to almost feel them and understand them in my mind in order to be able to draw them. I took the liberty of making the statue at least three times bigger than it actually is so that it would not be as dwarfed by the advertisements as it is in reality.

I was so pleased by this painting that I made my daughter Naomi a little *Eros* card for her twenty-first birthday.

When I moved to London in 1966, I lived near the Portobello Road and we used to walk up and down that area a lot. I have always loved seeing people move, how they do it. I loved the shop windows. Although I knew my place was in the city, I didn't understand then how I could use it and give my living environment a place in the studio. I know now that what I want to say is, "Hey. Look. Living in a city is wonderful, something to be proud of. Enjoy it."

The Gatwick Express paintings

When I was first asked to do a painting of London, the Houses of Parliament and the River Thames immediately came to mind and I spent many an early morning, when the water was calm, thinking and meditating and researching images of this area. I was smitten with the subject matter, and this is one of two paintings and a print that developed at this time.

Westminster [1996]
Acrylic on canvas, 101.6 x 63.5 cm

I considered Harrods as a possible subject for this series and whilst I was outside one day I became aware of the taxis queuing up and took some photographs of them. It was only later when I was looking through all the information I had collected that I realised a taxi was something I would like to paint, not only because of its unique shape, but also its special sound; when I look at the painting it is almost as if I can hear the clunk of the diesel engine, which is very important for me. It is a unique and bold painting.

Taxis [1996]
Acrylic on canvas, 101.6 x 63.5 cm

This commission from English Heritage arose for their year of Christian Heritage. I went to Canterbury to see the ruined Abbey. There is a magnificent aura even though there is so little of the building left. Remaining features include a window and a few pillars, and graves with wonderful old English names on them. Since Catholicism is my background I have an inkling of the tradition of the abbeys and what happened to them, and I went back and forth for several days trying to assimilate the spirit of the place. At one stage someone walked out of the site saying, "Why should I pay to see just a few stones? There is nothing there." They had missed the point. It is not a place to gossip in or idle time away. You have to go in calmly and be prepared to walk slowly on your own to experience it.

The ruined form was so simple and direct that there had to be more to make the painting work. What I decided to use was texture. The stone was quite crumbly. It was soft and rich and I felt it would erode if I rubbed it. There is a lot of free painting in this canvas because to get the right quality for the stone, I had to use fairly thick, liquid paint. Half the painting is the stone and the arch and the other half is the sky, which I felt gave it a religious connotation, like the Light of the World coming through the Triumphal Arch.

St Augustine's Abbey [1996]
Acrylic on canvas, 101.6 x 63.5 cm

Brookland Heights [1996]
Acrylic on canvas, 121.9 x 177.8 cm

This was a commission from Aukett, the architects of this award-winning headquarters for Procter & Gamble, on the site where Stirling Moss and other drivers used to race. The painting had to be done in an extremely short time and I worked day and night on it so that it could be included in the Royal Academy of Arts' Summer Exhibition.

The building is a simple box with a bold interior-exterior, achieved through setting all the offices around an immense atrium. The painting took its starting point from a corner of the atrium and I tried to make it as light and rich as possible – which is why the blues and whites and creams are so intense – because the main impact of the building is that it is so light-filled that you almost feel you are in the open air.

The painting now hangs in the atrium that is its subject matter. If I am doing a commission of this nature, I want people to love and appreciate the building they are in more and I want to help that happen by using my vision to suggest perspectives they may not have seen before or by encouraging them to look harder.

The Creek, Dubai [1996]
Acrylic on paper, 52 x 38 cm

Having visited Dubai several times and seen how important the Creek is – it divides one side from the other – and been intrigued by the dhows loaded with goods and all the life and activity on the water, I was inspired to work from it. The boats are huge, hulking things, made of wood and the particular one that appears in the painting is used in an abstract way, so that the rudder and back end of the boat break into the overall surface and are reflected by it. It is almost as though the disturbance in the water has formed its own language, which relates to the patterns used so widely to decorate the windows of buildings in that part of the world. This so intrigued me that I was to follow this visual idea in the *Old Souq* painting (page 152).

Sheraton, Dubai [1996]
Acrylic on paper, 38 x 52 cm

Unlike most of my paintings, this one uses artificial light as an important part of its subject matter and that in itself captures something important about Dubai, which is very contemporary and man-made. The painting happened by accident. I was on my second or third visit to Dubai and was beginning to feel as if I knew the place a little, and had some feeling for it and so I was quite consciously looking for imagery that I might paint. I had arranged to meet someone at the hotel and went up the escalator and saw an area that summed up, not only the glitter and the fabulous riches of the place, but also the golden colour of the

sun on the sand which is all around the city.

The painting uses a section of the lift shaft, but that is not important in terms of the overall subject matter, which was the shimmer and quality of the whole environment. It has a watery feel, although there is no water in the image, and there is almost the sense of being there and not there at the same time. There was in fact a beautiful fountain in the area below the picture but it didn't interest me. Colour and richness were the motivating factors.

Sheraton, Dubai is glittery and golden, a warm painting. It is a little like the mysteries of the East.

The Dubrovnik paintings

I was among a group of six Royal Academicians who were invited to Dubrovnik to make some work for a joint exhibition in the Academy, the proceeds of which were to help the Monuments' Appeal in Croatia.

I took pencils, paints and pads. My bedroom window overlooked the sea (which lapped the sides of our hotel) and the view would have made a terrific postcard. I began drawing, but it was a waste of time because I was not getting to know what made Dubrovnik tick. In the end what I did was walk and walk and walk within the city walls. I trod everything so many times I surmise I know it better than many people who live there. I needed to know and feel and understand what I wanted, before I painted. Often it helps to know the history of the place you are painting and I was introduced to a guide and said to her, "I just want to listen". She talked non-stop for four or five hours, illuminating the places I had already discovered.

The final series of paintings is made up from details of various aspects I had seen. They are relatively small works on paper but the odd thing is, it takes as long to do a 2-foot by 20-inch painting as it does to do one 30-foot by 8. I used acrylic on good heavyweight paper. As I wanted the same sort of light and heat, I worked on some of them in my studio in France.

The first painting, *Dubrovnik*, was looking through the city walls onto the Adriatic, which is an incredibly beautiful sea. I wanted the darkness and thickness of the wall with the sparkling rich blue, quivering light-filled sea beyond it. You cannot get away from water in Dubrovnik, it is around half of the city. With this painting, I became aware of the importance of the texture of the walls and stone. It puzzled me and fed into the rest of the series. It was the first time in a long while that I had been so concerned with texture and consciously made it part of the content, even the subject matter. The series is partly about the tactile quality of *Dubrovnik*.

Within the walls there are two delightful monasteries, offering peace from the bustle and activity of the city. The light in the Franciscan seminary and in the monastery gardens was distilled and very quiet compared to the main square, where it is very stark, or

to the rippling light on the sea which you can sit and look at for ages. I wanted to prepare material from one of the monasteries and I chose a window area, with shadow and dappled light going across a wall. Tonally, this painting goes from light to quite dark, and when I was working on it, I almost didn't push it far enough because I was frightened the light would be too light, and the dark too dark. In fact, in that environment there was nothing too dark or too light; it was black and white, extraordinary. Oddly enough, the work relates to the *Old Souq* (page 152) painting; when I was looking at the souk it was with Dubrovnik in mind. This one is much stronger in terms of structure; the souk painting is camouflaged in comparison.

Another image, *City Wall*, came from the visits I made every evening to a café next to St. Blaise Cathedral. I made studies based on a huge rock ball carved on a plinth, behind which is a pillar-shaped structure attached to one of the buildings. I was not trying to make it representational, only to make sure that the qualities and concept were there, and that they could be understood by the viewer. That painting is very much to do with the stone and rock of the area and how the light hits it. Within the city everything seems to be hewn out of rock, and to have a great presence and weight to it. In *Fountain* there is a strange lightness, and it seems as though it has been moulded from the rock. I was glad I had walked and walked because it meant that I had all the memories when I was in the studio, and the experience dictated the quality and aura of the paintings. It was as if I was touching the stone and bricks and was still there.

There is an island within the bay to which I had been as a student in 1964. It has quite a history, a fort and a castle and a botanical garden so I had decided to revisit it. There is no coastal road and it was a particularly windy day, so bad that I thought we were going to sink; I was petrified going back. That evening, however, we had a stunning sunset and I did studies for two skyscapes based on it. We don't get sunsets like that in Britain, the sun goes into a huge red ball and suddenly hurtles down and disappears and it is dark.

Dubrovnik [1996]
Acrylic on paper, 52 x 38 cm

The Dubrovnik paintings

City Wall [1996]
Acrylic on paper, 52 x 38 cm

Fountain [1996]
Acrylic on paper, 52 x 38 cm

The Dubrovnik paintings

Sky Over Dubrovnik [1996]
Acrylic on paper, 52 x 38 cm

Dusk, Dubrovnik [1996]
Acrylic on paper, 52 x 38 cm

The Old Souq, Dubai [1996]
Acrylic on paper, 52 x 38 cm

This painting was based on memories of my trips to Dubai and Sharjah. In both cases, the old souqs have been redeveloped since I first went and I wanted to capture the spirit of the old ways of bartering in the marketplaces before the changes. On my first visits, there had been scruffy back streets and dark parlours but now there is a new order which has altered the ways in which trading is done.

I spent several days collecting material, walking and walking round Dubai souq. On one particular day it was virtually empty, and it was that quietness and solitude which I wanted to put in the picture. I based the image on a wall across which shadows from a bougainvillaea were cast in the strong sun; I wanted a sense of age, timelessness and heat. I liked the way the light dappled the wall more than the tree itself, and I was able to play with the shadows and leaf shapes to make something far more interesting than just the plain wall, which was not in fact very beautiful. Although this painting was triggered by reality, it evolved more from memory.

I used the spray gun so that the dots would be more visible than usual, and would give the feeling of stone and rock to make the façade almost tangible. The dots have a presence and are slightly raised from the rest of the painting. Technique is part of my craft; I am in control of it and I make it work for me but I don't want it to dominate. The imagery and content are the important elements, not the way they are achieved.

This painting was commissioned by Loughborough University. I spent two or three days on the campus and decided to use the Pilkington Library as the starting place for the painting, because it is the central point of the university. I was concerned to create a strong structure, and gradually the composition took over and made demands that removed it slightly from the actual building. For instance, in reality the windows don't go down to the ground, they are small; for the painting's sake I have extended them. Although the architecture has some richness, I wanted to make a striking powerful painting so I have given the pillars far more detail than they have themselves.

It is a figurative painting but it has to work as an abstraction. The concrete supports that go up the outside of the building occupy a vast area of the canvas. Three-quarters of the painting is to do with the surface and quality of the materials it is built from. I found it intriguing to make the large cream area diverse enough to hold the eye's attention. Within the surface there are shifts and shadows and that has allowed me to push the browns and ochres (unusual colours for me) as much as possible and to warm and cool them with blues, oranges and reds. The bottom quarter uses the windows and their reflective qualities and creates a contrast with the weight of the areas above it. It is a spacious campus and I wanted a sense of that to be included, which I hope happens in the lower part; there is a hint of sky in the reflections, which also pick up the trees and houses. The blue is strong and startling because of the tonality of the rest of the work.

When I am doing a commission, it must be accepted that I will change things as I see fit. It is my eye that decides what will work, not an architectural plan or a design. In a sense this was a typical commission. If I had been to Loughborough I would not have said, "I must paint that." Having been given the commission, I was really pleased. Commissions can push you to do things you might not have considered before. I learnt from doing this one and it provided something powerful for me.

Loughborough [1997]
Acrylic on canvas, 182.9 x 137.2 cm

The atmosphere of this painting is one of lightness and airiness and when I was making it I kept on thinking of the delicacy, movement and flow of a ballet dancer. This was particularly ironic as I had injured my foot and felt welded to the floor! In a strange way, the hurt of my body was counteracted by the pleasure I took in the agility of the painting, and I was probably all the more aware of its floating qualities than I would otherwise have been.

The commission came from the architects of the building, Aukett, and the site is near to Heathrow Airport. I was anxious not to overload the work with details and wanted to keep to the barest, uncluttered elements.

Clockhouse Stairwell [1997]
Acrylic on canvas, 182.9 x 137.2 cm

As in many cities with rivers, the Creek plays and important part in the life of Dubai. I brought this into the painting, using the image created by the light of the late afternoon sun rippling across the water. With each visit I made to the city I became more alert to the enormous changes going on there. It is impossible not to respond to its modernity.

I liked the idea of dividing the canvas; in one sense the subject matter had been reduced, the size of the painting narrowed. The pillar, however, is integral to the painting, with its own character, colour and markings and is no less important for its simplicity.

Creekside [1997]
Acrylic on canvas, 76.2 x 61 cm

Listening to the Light

In the various interviews about his work which Brendan Neiland (born Lichfield, 1941) has given up to now, two early experiences seem seminal. Firstly, Neiland has spoken about how, when he was a young boy, he lived in the country: initially Norfolk, and then Suffolk. When, aged 14, he moved to Birmingham, the shock he got – a positive one, in terms of what the mature artist has called 'the scale, the richness of everything' – was enormous. The interplay of cloudscape and skyscraper, of city and countryside, has remained a constant factor in his work. A few years later, Neiland left Birmingham to study for the priesthood in a Catholic seminary. The studies only lasted two years, but the effect on Neiland was profound: not so much in terms of the impact of any theological dogma, but rather, in terms of the life-long respect which these years instilled in him for the necessity of developing and sustaining faith in one's activity. In other words, a faith to be rooted in the discipline of exacting, arduous – and ultimately rewarding – work.

The Superior at the Seminary encouraged Neiland's early interest in art: the young student painted stage sets as well as large heads for Saints' Feasts days. As the artist himself has remarked, he was thus introduced early on to the idea of working in a large and public manner. Upon leaving the Seminary, Neiland took his Diploma in Art and Design at the Art College in Birmingham. He remembers the three years which he spent there as being as inspirational as they were exciting. The work of tutors such as John Walker and Ivor Abrahams epitomised the fruits of what Neiland experienced as a refreshing, even revolutionary approach to Fine Art education. The emphasis was firmly upon matters of self-discovery and expression, rather than any academic subservience to the rigours of the life-model class (rigours which, as a teacher, Neiland has subsequently come to value highly).

During these early years in Birmingham, Neiland experienced a creative tension between his love of (the then highly fashionable) American Abstract Expressionism and his growing need to find a strong, ostensible subject matter for his work. What first helped give shape to Neiland's early artistic ideas and ambitions were the factories and foundries of Birmingham, and in particular, the extraordinary presence which Neiland sensed in the painted ships' propellors which he was able to see created during a few weeks' work in a factory. He recalls this as an experience which would shortly lead him towards the use of a spray gun technique.

At this time, appropriately enough, the ex-would-be priest was beginning to appreciate the work of Fernand Léger, one of the high priests of a socially-oriented Modernism. A visit to the great Cubist collector Douglas Cooper, at his château just outside Avignon, did much to develop Neiland's taste for Léger, an artist whose work he had at first sight considered 'quite repulsive', but which he quickly came to appreciate. During the latter part of his Diploma years, Neiland's studio walls would feature one Léger print or reproduction after another, as his interest in the Norman's mastery of the relations of post-Cubist object-forms and boldly conceived pictorial planes, harmonised through liberated yet rigorously structured colour relations, grew apace.

Upon graduation from Birmingham, Neiland went to the Royal College of Art, immediately following the generation of David Hockney, R. B. Kitaj and Peter Blake. He studied here from 1966 to 1969. Much as one might wish to question aspects of the popular mythology of 'swinging London' to which these times gave birth, the impact of London upon the young graduate must have been enormous. Neiland himself recalls an extraordinary range of stimulation. This ranged from music (a multi-genre passion which continues to this day) and a host of exhibitions (with Neiland experiencing a growing appreciation of both British and American Pop Art) to a fast-increasing awareness of the beauty implicit within the reflective surface of a car bonnet or shop window. Neiland's attention was also caught by the rich variety of forms available to the artistically curious eye at the Science Museum. During his time at the Royal College, he made hundreds upon hundreds of drawings, developing his feeling for and command of the relations of part and whole, positive and negative space through endless studies of various machine parts, cars and aeroplanes.

Just as Léger's various hymns to Modernity had avoided any hint of overworked impasto, so did Neiland quickly come to realise that the artistic realisation of his particular perception of the object – whether machine part or car headlight – demanded a high, flat finish. Much to the consternation of the Painting School professor, Carel Weight, whom Neiland otherwise remembers as 'a magnificent professor, as well as a magnificent painter', he ordered a compressor and spray gun and made his first experiments with the exacting technique of which he has subsequently become such a patient and extraordinary master.

Shortly afterwards, Neiland's concept of drawing was to be considerably enlarged by his increasing use of photography – a medium that he continues to use (with discrimination) today. The camera, as he puts it, has become his sketchbook. No matter how scrupulous the research in that sketchbook might be, the aim has never been to serve any direct notion of topographical representation. Neiland's purpose with the camera is, rather, to stimulate the creativity of an increasingly acute and synthesizing pictorial intelligence. This is an intelligence which has been able to make increasingly subtle – yet bold – art out of the relations of such elements as geometrical grid and curvilinear silhouette; saturated colour field (both energetic and contemplative in effect) and variously angled line; grainy, film-like surfaces and delicate, dappled hues; strong, cropped forms and mirrored, Cubist-like ambiguity. Exploring the tensions and the transmutations of the conceptual and the painterly, mimesis and (re)presentation, abstraction and figuration, Neiland's variously distilled meditations upon the contemporary cityscape have come to project a unique atmosphere – at once intimate and grand, celebratory and melancholy.

Since his postgraduate studies, Neiland's commitment to the work ethic instilled in him in his seminary days has paid increasingly rewarding dividends. Quickly noted as one of the most interesting of the second generation of British artists to engage with aspects of mass culture, his very particular, intensely focused approach to the dialectic of photographic (re)presentation and the multi-layered painted and printed image drew the favourable attention of such noted British critics as Marina Vaizey, William Packer and Edward Lucie-Smith, with the last-named featuring him in his 1970 book 'Art in Britain' as well as in such subsequent publications as the 1979 'Super Realism'. Neiland has continued to exhibit consistently, widely and successfully, achieving particular recognition for the work he has executed with the London master printer Brad Faine. There have been commissions from a distinguished range of corporate clients in Britain and abroad, the work often featuring the soaring glass and steel structures typical of our era's commercial architecture. There has also been recognition at the highest professional level: Neiland was elected to the Royal Academy in 1992 and made Professor of Painting at the University of Brighton in 1996.

It is to Neiland's great credit that, at the same time that his work has been able to satisfy a diverse range of corporate briefs, his artistry has increasingly evinced a relation (sometimes implicit, sometimes explicit) with key formal and spiritual aspects of the Western painting tradition. It has long been a shibboleth of much 20th-century Modernist art that, should one wish to express something at least of the depths of life's potentialities, one must somehow rupture the surface of existence, the better to reveal – for example – archetypal mythic material (Gorky and Pollock) or various possible parallels between avant-garde art and science (Kandinsky and Klee). In Neiland, the opposite obtains: close observance of – and respect for – the seeming surface of things may conjure doubly reflective planes of perception and poetry, feeling and imagination. It is the essentially luminous interplay of surface and depth, near and far that links Neiland's art to central aspects of Western painting history.

From the early Renaissance – as Paul Hills has documented in his exemplary study 'The Light of Early Italian Painting' – to Claude and Turner, Velasquez and Vermeer, the Impressionists and beyond, the diverse interplay of naturalistic and divine conceptions of light has provided the (variegated) conceptual ground of the poetics of Western painting. In a century which has often – all too hastily – proclaimed its divorce from certain traditional aspects of the spiritual or the sacred, Neiland has created work upon work where light functions in an enigmatic, spiritually intriguing and energising manner. Intimating the depths of both late 20th-century alienation and timeless (yet timebound) longing contained within a moment's reflection – in the mystery of mirrored light, held in creative equipoise between worlds of culture and nature, technology and spirit – Neiland's art can bridge the sacred and the profane realms, in a manner at once formally striking and perceptually – psychologically – subtly understated.

What one might call the mature 'Neiland effect' lies in both such a bridging of realms and the work's simultaneous appeal to the public and the private domains. This is realised through the marriage of an essentially Modernist reduction of narrative or anecdotal concerns with an engaging, undogmatic openness of technical means and 'meaning'. No matter how conceptually or technically thorough the work may be (and few other contemporary artists offer such thoroughly realised images) this is an art open to interpretation, to the creative participation of the spectator. How, then, might we best begin to appreciate Neiland's art? Acknowledging the force of Braque's insight that the truly valuable thing about a work of art is that aspect of it which cannot be verbalised, we may nonetheless try to come a little closer to the enigmatic core of Neiland's œuvre by considering some of the

chief elements of thematic ambiguity which are to be discerned within such an ostensibly upfront art of surface and reflection: of charged consumerist object and meditative space, of imposing, translucent architecture and distant, cloud-flecked skies.

While people themselves never appear in Neiland's pictures, their presence is in fact everywhere, implicit in the pictures' variously mediated evidence of their labour – whether this be the sexually-charged curve of a car headlamp or bumper, the soaring fenestration of a skyscraper or the sweep of a railway station concourse. And while Neiland is rightly seen as an interpreter of contemporary life, above all of the city, one should remember those aspects of his art which embrace a sense of history – whether that history involves the architectural legacy of Georgian *Bath* (1992) or the Orientalist fantasies of *Brighton Pavilion* (1993), the ruins of *St Augustine's Abbey* (1996) or the war-torn view of *Dubrovnik* (1996). As the collage-like contrasts of light and shade, the bold, simplified forms and austere pictorial rigour of the last-named work make particularly evident, Neiland's engagement with history has nothing to do with matters of either documentary reportage or historical moralising.

Modernist that he (in good part) is, sensitive to such formal matters as the (post-Cubist) integrity of the picture plane and the essential need, as Braque once put it, to eschew anecdote for the demands of a pictorial event, Neiland is open-minded enough to allow aspects of essentially pre-Modernist linear and aerial perspective into his work, if and when the need for such factors arises. Contemporary as the work manifestly is, there is a refreshing absence of the historically driven, or socio-politically determined, in these images. Certainly, there is but little sense of that patented-leather 'heroism of everyday life' which the 19th-century poet and critic Charles Baudelaire believed it the duty of the painter of modern city life to render epic. One senses that Neiland might be much more sympathetic to the reveries of Baudelaire's mysterious, cloud-loving stranger than to the programmatic imperatives of any such manifesto.

However – and here the enigma deepens – a good deal

of Neiland's work could clearly be viewed in the light of that post-Baudelairian Utopian tradition epitomised by the synthesizing, post-Cubist ambitions and achievements of Fernand Léger – an important early influence on the artist, as we have seen – or the 'simultaneity' of structural and temporal effect cultivated by Robert and Sonia Delaunay. At the same time, what Neiland has called 'the muted richness' he would wish his art to contain can suggest very different realms of experience. Some way from the celebratory worlds of Léger and the Delaunays, Neiland's subtle transitions of colour and various interweavings of reflected and refracted form can strike – or rather, intimate – the sort of quietly disquieting note redolent of certain moments of enigmatic displacement, or metaphysical unease, in artists as diverse as Edward Hopper (a painter for whom Neiland feels no small affinity), the young Giorgio de Chirico or René Magritte.

Neiland himself likes to emphasise that, whether one thinks of New York or Paris, London or Brighton, his own experiences of city and town have led to a search for a vision very distant from what he calls 'the concrete surfaces, the unpleasantness' of a good deal of contemporary urban existence. It remains the case, nonetheless, that should we choose to see them as such, a good number of Neiland's paintings and prints can sustain the sort of socio-political interpretation which would see in their predominantly cool tones and spacious, empty atriums a poignant adumbration of the alienation of much late 20th-century life, as experienced under the high-tech gloss of either state socialism or corporate capitalism. This is a theme already present in the architectural eclipsing of humanity characteristic of the New York photographs of Paul Strand, in work roughly contemporary with that of Léger and the Delaunays, but it is a theme which Neiland makes very much his own. In Neiland, humanity is simultaneously present (despite its physical absence) and hauntingly absent (despite its technologically mediated presence).

The ambiguous, open-ended quality of Neiland's art is further reinforced when one remembers that, much as this art demands to be seen in the light of ideas associated with the development of painting and photography in the modern city, it is also intimately related to central aspects of the mood and manner of the British, European and Scandinavian tradition of Romantic landscape painting. Contemplating both the floating evanescence and palpable weight of Neiland's beautiful *Cloudscapes* (1991) it is only natural that the many early 19th-century cloud studies of John Constable and the Norwegian Johan Christian Dahl should come to mind. This is an association also evoked by a good many of Neiland's spiritually-oriented, predominantly Northern landscapes of the mid-to late-1990s, exemplified by the 1995 ScotRail commission *Loch Shiel*. Here, the foreground – yet distanced, off-centre – silhouette of the Bonnie Prince Charlie monument offers a rare instance of the human figure in Neiland's art, supplying mute, humble yet dignified counterpoint to the vastness of the vista beyond.

On the one hand then, Neiland is clearly the painter who has done the most to transform the Impressionists' obsession with the poetry and the poetics of the bourgeois city – think only of Monet's various celebrations of railway steam and station, or of Pissarro's boldy conceived series of post-Haussmann boulevard vistas – into the stuff of late 20th-century life and art. On the other hand, one must acknowledge that Neiland is also an artist who has done much to remind us of the continuing relevance of essentially Romantic themes of landscape and light, sometimes picturesque, sometimes sublime. Like the German Gerhard Richter (but with different intentions and, broadly speaking, different results) he has had the courage to venture into areas that have long been under threat of pollution from kitsch.

One does not have to be especially literate in the theory or the politics of either democracy or deep ecology to sense how important it is today that the nature-sensitive message of someone like the late Joseph Beuys is transmitted in dimensions other than the purely conceptual or performance-based: that a commercially successful pictorial artist like Neiland continues to offer us work which is able to stimulate our sense of the grandeur of the natural world. At the same time, the sheer range of Neiland's work places that sensitivity to the natural world within an appropriately complex context.

In a recent intriguing essay entitled 'Landscape as Experience and Vision', published to accompany the 1993 exhibition 'Towards A New Landscape' which took place at the Bernard Jacobson Gallery, London, the art historian Norbert Lynton examined various aspects of the survival and development of a sensitivity to nature (as manifest within the British landscape tradition) in the late 20th century. Focusing on the evolving tensions between rural and urban themes within his subject, Lynton concluded that Modernist dreams of Utopian city life have long been soured by the realities of urban decay and violence. However, the urban-driven advances of electronically-based contemporary communications have ensured that rural existence need never again imply a life lived in isolation from that quickened, multiple consciousness which is often taken to represent the best of city-based culture. We need, observes Lynton, a new kind of painting, to help us to grasp the potentialities of a future where city and countryside are no longer seen as polar – and clichéd – opposites. The art of Brendan Neiland speaks precisely of such a development.

As we have seen, Neiland has at times been characterised as a Super Realist. However, as the critic Marina Vaizey has observed, it is perhaps of only limited value to relate this artist's work to such a generalising art-historical label. As Vaizey points out, and as this essay has been concerned to argue, the essential thing about Neiland is the highly individual territory to which he has staked a claim. In a work like the 1993 *Riverside* – to which we shall shortly return – that territory is especially evident, speaking of the sort of many-sided, historically subtle and experientially fluid sense of reality which takes Neiland's work quite some way from that of American Super Realists like Richard Estes or Robert Cottingham (a distinction drawn by Lucie-Smith in his 1979 'Super Realism').

In his 1991 study 'Art Since Mid-Century', the art historian Daniel Wheeler has suggested that the cleverly constructed, multiple city vistas of Estes (born 1936)

transport the spirit of Vermeer (as embodied, presumably, in such a work as the c. 1661 *View of Delft*) into the late 20th century. Wheeler has a point. However, it has always seemed to me it is in the variously blue-saturated work of Neiland that a more suggestive contemporary relation to aspects of Vermeer might be found. In Neiland the sweeping, all-inclusive vista of Estes gives way to the cropped yet expansive fragment, a fragment that intimates – rather than represents – aspects of an ultimately mysterious totality. As in Vermeer (long one of Neiland's chief elective affinities) a poetic distillation of object-relations summons thematic ambiguity, as elements of pictorial and psychological simplicity and complexity combine in the service of a light-suffused dialectic of interior and exterior spatial experience. Not only that: in such works of Neiland's as *Turbulence* (a marvellously enigmatic work, and one of his finest achievements), *Rhythmic Reflections* and *Gliding Light* (all from 1992) one can sense how much Neiland has absorbed and made new that painstaking attention to matters of (clear yet multivalent) pictorial structure and space which is as evident in Braque, for example, as it is (in very different guise) in Vermeer.

A good deal of Neiland's work demands to be seen, not so much in terms of its relation to that of a contemporary American like Estes, but rather – as has already been suggested – with regard to its relation to aspects of the evolving poetics of European painting, as epitomised by such central figures as Vermeer and Corot, Léger and Braque. With regard to the last-named, think of Neiland's relation to the archetypal theme of the window within a painting, as treated by Braque in his 1939 *L'Atelier Au Tabouret*, for example. Here there are both rhythmic structures and tonal values – albeit not a quality of touch – very much in line with aspects of Neiland's later explorations. And if Neiland's art can, on one level, be seen as a sort of late 20th-century equivalent to and development of the Impressionists' focus on the blurred details of 19th-century city life and landscape, then one should also consider the relation of aspects of his art to that of the man to whom – as Monet certainly knew – the Impressionists owed so much, and whom Delacroix once called 'a rare genius and the father of modern landscape': Jean Baptiste Camille Corot.

Landscapes of Corot's such as the 1864 *Recollection of Mortefontaine* or the 1873 *Pond at Ville-d'Avray with Leaning Tree* have long been admired for their enchanting blend of the ethereal and the material, the observed and the imagined: the whole united by the sort of subtly silvered luminosity that conveys what a post-Kandinsky sensibility would call the 'inner sound' – or the harmonious musicality – of the motif. There have been several late 20th-century painters who have paid either implicit or explict homage to Corot: one thinks, for example, of a good many of the recent watercolours of Ian Potts, or of Howard Hodgkin's *After Corot* of 1979-82. However, few contemporary artists have come as close to Corot as Neiland has done in parts of the simultaneously liquescent and aerial atmospherics, the lucid geometries and fugitive reflections of *Riverside*. Completely of the late 20th century in the interwoven complexity of its elements, the poetry which is *Riverside* exemplifies the manner in which Neiland's multi-layered art can offer a deeply satisfying blend of the contemporary and the historical, technology and nature, the earth-bound and the ascensional, the tangible and the ineffable.

In conclusion, one might attempt to summarise the enigma of Neiland's art thus: on one level, much of Neiland's œuvre deals with both the sophisticated steel and glass structures of modern (and post-modern) city architecture, and the similarly developed sensibilities of those viewers who are able to sense that twin dialectic of the (disguised) topographical and the typical, the abstracted and the representational, which is so consistently woven into the work. On another level – the level which Kandinsky addressed when he spoke of the 'inner sound' which the musicality of a spiritually inspiring painting should generate, in order to prevent its becoming simply decorative – Neiland's art embraces the sort of questions which throughout the ages have exercised poets and painters, philosophers and theologians alike. Contemplating the light-saturated grandeur of some of Neiland's images of railway concourses, for example, we may sense that the journey

to be imagined is not necessarily to be found on any train timetable.

If what captures light belongs to what it captures; if light is both the object and agent of vision: then what – or who – is the (ultimate) source of that vision? If, as in so much of Neiland's art, the details of life – the architecture of existence – can be experienced in terms of rhythmic pattern, or an essentially musical harmony, of what do that pattern and harmony sing? If the evanescent and the ineffable are only to be captured in the artifice of art, what vision of life might such artifice stimulate? Are we ever to assuage – or abandon – our nostalgia for the infinite?

As an artist, Brendan Neiland is, of course, under no obligation to answer any such questions. On the contrary: a large part of his achievement has been to refresh and replenish the means by which such questions might float into consciousness, precipitating not answers, but rather our creative participation in the more mysterious moments of life – in the poetics of perception. At his best, as this essay has been concerned to demonstrate, Neiland is considerably closer to Vermeer or Corot, Braque or Léger than he is, for example, to an American contemporary like Estes (or Estes's Super Realist compatriots, Robert Cottingham and Ralph Goings). In an art at once social and solitary, rigorous and open-ended, Brendan Neiland offers a uniquely distilled range of reflections both of and upon contemporary life: reflections of lasting import, born as they are from the patient deliberations of a sensibility that would listen to – and exalt – the language of light.

Dr Michael Tucker
Michael Tucker (born Warrington, 1948) is Professor of Poetics at the University of Brighton. In 1997 the University of Sussex awarded him the degree of Doctor of Letters. Author of the acclaimed 'Dreaming With Open Eyes: The Shamanic Spirit in Twentieth-Century Art and Culture' (HarperCollins, London 1992), his publications feature material on a range of contemporary artists and musicians, including Alan Davie and Ian McKeever, Frans Widerberg and Jan Garbarek.

Biographical Notes

Important Dates

1941   Born Lichfield, Stafford

1962-66 Attended Birmingham College of Art

1966-69 Attended Royal College of Art, London

1970   Joined Angela Flowers Gallery, London

1979   Joined Fischer Fine Art, London

1992   Joined The Redfern Gallery, London

1992   Elected Royal Academician

1996   Elected Fellow of the Royal Society of Arts
          Appointed Professor of Painting, University of Brighton

Awards

1965   Phipps Bequest Scholarship

1966   Louisa Ann Ryland Scholarship

1968   The Contemporary Art Society Purchase Prize,
          Northern Young Contemporaries

1969   Arthur Tooth Prize, Young Contemporaries
          Silver Medal, Royal College of Art
          John Minton Scholarship

1972   Arts Council of Great Britain Award

1978   John Moores XI Prize Winner

1989   Daler-Rowney Award, Royal Academy of Arts
          Summer Exhibition, London

1996   Best Use of Illustration in an Advertisement
          for the Highland Collection –
          Scottish Advertising & Design Award, Edinburgh

Exhibitions

One-Man Exhibitions

1971   - Angela Flowers Gallery, London

1972   - Angela Flowers Gallery, London

1973   - Victoria and Albert Museum, London - Travelling Exhibition

1974   - Angela Flowers Gallery, London

1976   - Brunel University, Uxbridge
          - Park Square Gallery, Leeds
          - Arts Council Gallery, Belfast
          - Angela Flowers Gallery, London
          - Oxford Gallery, Oxford

1977   - Eastern Arts Tour, The Minories, Colchester
          - *Prints and Paintings on Paper.* AIR Gallery, London

1979   - Fischer Fine Art Gallery, London

1980   - Polytechnic Art Gallery, Newcastle

1981   - Print Show, Anderson O'Day Gallery, London,

          - Bury St Edmunds Gallery, Bury St Edmunds

1983   - Drumcroon Gallery, Wigan Education Art Centre, Wigan

1984   - Fischer Fine Art, London

1987   - Anderson O'Day Gallery, London

1988   - The Parnham Trust, Dorset
          - Archive Display of the work in creating the print *Lloyd's*. The Tate Gallery, London.

1989   - *Painting Beyond Architecture - Independent Observation.* Royal Institute of British Architects Galleries, London

1991   - *Recent Paintings Brendan Neiland.* Fischer Fine Art Gallery, London

1992   - Gardner Centre, Brighton
          - Milton Keynes Exhibition Centre, Milton Keynes
          - Northern Centre for Contemporary Art, Sunderland
          - Stafford Art Gallery, Stafford
          - Drumcroon Arts Centre, Wigan
          - Nottingham University Arts Centre, Nottingham
          - Grundy Art Gallery, Blackpool

1993   - The Redfern Gallery, London
          - Reading College of Arts & Technology, Reading

1994   - University of Brighton, Brighton

1994-95 - *A Display of Prints and Working Materials 1974-94.* Royal Academy of Arts, London

1995   - *Highlights: New Screen Prints.* Lamont Gallery, London

1996   - *Cityscapes & Landscape.* Pallant House, Chichester

1997   - *Brendan Neiland RA – On Reflection, Paintings Drawings and Prints.* The Redfern Gallery, London
          - Friends' Room, Royal Academy of Arts, London
          - University of Brighton, Brighton

1998   - Loughborough University, Loughborough
          - Keele University, Keele

Group Exhibitions

1969   - *Young Contemporaries*, London
          - *Young and Fantastic.* ICA Galleries, The Mall, London
          - *Big Pictures for Public Places.* Royal Academy of Arts, London

1970   - Bradford Print Biennale, Bradford
          - Open Painting Exhibition, Belfast, Northern Ireland

1971   - *Big Pictures for Public Places.* Whitworth Gallery, Manchester

1972   - *Photography into Art.* Camden Arts Centre, London
          - Bradford Print Biennale, Bradford

1973   - *Immagini Come Strumente di Realta.* Galleria la Citta, Verona, Italy
          - Industrial Sponsors Exhibition, Peterborough and London
          - *Five New Paintings.* Angela Flowers Gallery, London
          - *An Octet from Angela Flowers.* Angela Flowers Gallery, London

1974   - Bradford Print Biennale, Bradford
          - *Five Painters.* Manchester City Art Gallery, Manchester
          - *Contemporary British Prints.* Brooklyn Museum, New York and subsequent American tour

1975   - Chichester National Art Exhibition, Chichester
          - *From Britain 75.* Helsinki, Finland
          - Contemporary Art Society Art Fair. Mall Galleries, London
          - *Reality, Mystery and Illusion.* Rochdale Art Gallery, Rochdale

1976
- *Angela Flowers 8*. Gulbenkian Gallery, Newcastle
- Bradford Print Biennale, Bradford
- *British Realists*. Icon Gallery, Birmingham
- Oliver Dowling Gallery, Dublin
- Arts Council Collection. Hayward Gallery, London

1977
- *Real Life*. Peter Moores Exhibition, Liverpool
- *Doors*. Camden Arts Centre, London
- *The Greater London Picture Show*. Angela Flowers Gallery, London
- *Works on Paper*. Contemporary Art Society, Royal Academy of Arts, London

1978
- *Working Processes*. A Sunderland Arts Touring Exhibition
- *The Figurative Approach 3*. Fischer Fine Art, London
- *Exposicion Internacional de la Plastica*. Santiago, Chile
- *Coriander Studios, Serigraphic Prints*. Curwen Gallery, London
- *Retrospectives*. Park Square Gallery, Leeds
- John Moores XI. Walker Art Gallery, Liverpool

1979
- Tolly Cobbold Eastern Arts Second National Exhibition. Fitzwilliam Museum, Cambridge and subsequent tour
- *Painters at Work*. National Theatre, London
- *Contemporary Art*. Mall Galleries, London
- Summer Exhibition. Royal Academy of Arts, London

1980
- *The Figurative Approach 4*. Fischer Fine Art , London
- Summer Exhibition. Royal Academy of Arts, London

1981
- *The Real British*. Fischer Fine Art, London
- *Artists into Print*. ICA Galleries, London
- 2nd Biennale of Graphical Art. Baden-Baden, Germany
- Summer Exhibition. Royal Academy of Arts, London

1982
- 7th British Print Biennale, Bradford
- *Presences of Nature* Cumbrian Landscape Exhibition. Carlisle Museum and subsequent tour
- *16 Artists at Battersea Arts Centre*, London
- The Richmond Studios, Brighton
- *Printmakers*. Drew Gallery, Canterbury
- *Screen Spectrum* Coriander Publications. Thumb Gallery, London
- Gallery Knoef, Holland
- *80 prints by Modern Masters*. Angela Flowers Gallery, London
- The Solomon Gallery, Dublin
- *Painter - Printmaker*. West Surrey College of Art & Design, Farnham
- *Snow*. Angela Flowers Gallery, London
- *Twelve by Twelve*. Leicestershire Museum & Art Gallery, Leicester
- Coriander Prints. Thumb Gallery, London

1983
- *Eight British Realists*. Louis K. Meisel Gallery, New York
- *Townscape Today*. Oldham Art Gallery, Oldham
- International Biennale of Graphic Art. Ljubljana, Slovenia
- *Pintura Britannica*. The Municipal Museum, Madrid
- *Words and Images of the Lake District*. Salford City Art Gallery, Salford
- *Recent Works*. Fischer Fine Art, London
- *Illustrative Images*. Collins Gallery, Glasgow
- *City Visions - Urban Landscape 1951-1980*. Bolton Art Gallery, Bolton
- *The Importance of Drawing*. West Surrey College of Art & Design, Farnham
- *The Music Show*. Thumb Gallery, London

1984
- *Printmaking-Making Prints*. Atkinson Art Gallery, Merseyside
- *Images et Imaginaires d'Architecture*. Centre Georges Pompidou, Paris
- *A Study in Patronage – Art Architecture and Design*, a two-man exhibition. Fischer Fine Art, London

1985
- *Summer in the City*. Icon Gallery, Birmingham
- *Some Aspects of British Landscape*. Fischer Fine Art, London
- *Visual Aid for Band Aid*. Royal Academy of Arts, London

1986
- 9th International Print Biennale. Cartwright Hall, Bradford City Art Gallery, Bradford
- *Boyd Bellany and Neiland*, Summer Show. Fischer Fine Art Gallery, London
- CAS Art Market. Smiths Galleries, London
- Opening and Mixed Exhibition. Anderson O'Day Gallery, London
- Summer Exhibition. Royal Academy of Arts, London

1987
- *Print Extravaganza*. Drumcroon Gallery, Wigan
- Summer Exhibition. Royal Academy of Arts, London
- Opening Group Show. Thumb Gallery, London
- 3rd International Biennial Print Exhibition: 1987 ROC Taipei Fine Arts Museum, Taiwan
- *Painting Prints, Sculptures*. Coach House Contemporary Art, Kirby Lonsdale

1988
- *Artists in National Parks*. Victoria and Albert Museum, London, followed in 1988-89 by a regional tour of British galleries and later to USA
- 150th Anniversary Painting Exhibition. Royal College of Arts, London
- Oxford Gallery, Oxford
- London Group, RCA Gallery, London
- Summer Exhibition. Royal Academy of Arts, London
- 112th Exhibition of Contemporary Prints. Bankside Gallery, London
- *Impressions of Cumbria*. Gallery North, Kirby Lonsdale
- *Print in a Day*. Bankside Gallery, London

1989
- *Printmaking From Britain*, Moscow
- *The President's Choice*. Royal Academy of Arts, London
- *A London Exhibition*. Fischer Fine Art, London
- *Images of Paradise*, an exhibition for Survival International, Harwood House, Yorkshire
- *The Advent Calendar*, a Contemporary View. Gallery North, Kirby Lonsdale
- 113th Exhibition of Contemporary Prints. Bankside Gallery, London
- Guest Exhibitor, New English Arts Club Open Exhibition. Mall Galleries, London
- Summer Exhibition. Royal Academy of Arts, London

1990
- *Directors' Choices*. The New Academy Gallery, London
- *Daniels, Harrison and Neiland in Leicestershire*. The City Gallery, Leicester
- *Artists in National Parks*. Houston International Festival, Oklahoma and Washington Meridian
- Summer Exhibition. Royal Academy of Arts, London
- *Accrochage*. Fischer Fine Art, London
- *The Discerning Eye*. Mall Galleries, London
- 114th Exhibition of Contemporary Prints. Bankside Gallery, London

1991
- Summer Exhibition. Royal Academy of Arts, London
- 115th Exhibition of Contemporary Prints. Bankside Gallery, London
- *The Discerning Eye*. Mall Galleries, London

1991-92 - *The Large Print Show*. Jill George Gallery, London

1992
- *The New Patrons*. National Art Collections Fund, Christies, London
- *British Art Comes to St Helena*. British Council Print Exhibition
- *Artists for Nuclear Disarmament*, London
- Summer Exhibition. The Redfern Gallery, London
- *Works on Paper*. Galerie Valerie, Knightsbridge, London
- *The Celebrated City*, Treasures from the Collection of the Corporation of London. Barbican Centre, London

- Summer Exhibition. Royal Academy of Arts, London
- *Art for a Fairer World (Oxfam)*, Glasgow, Cardiff and London

1993
- Summer Exhibition, Royal Academy of Arts, London
- *A Print is a Print*, Coriander Studio Exhibition. Cork Street Gallery, London

1994
- Summer Exhibition. Royal Academy of Arts, London
- Summer Show. The Redfern Gallery, London
- *Three British Artists*. Redpath Gallery, Vancouver
- *National Print Exhibition*. Mall Galleries, London

1995
- *A Taste of Art*. The Mirage, Dubai, United Arab Emirates
- *Brighton Since the Sixties*. University of Brighton Gallery, Brighton
- Summer Exhibition. Royal Academy of Arts, London
- Invited Artists NEAC Annual Show. Mall Galleries, London
- *William Gear Past and Present Friends*. Birmingham Museum and Art Gallery, Birmingham
- *Thirty Years of Northern Young Contemporaries*. Whitworth Art Gallery, Manchester
- *Contemporary Print Show*. Concourse Gallery, Barbican Arts Centre, London
- *National Print Exhibition*. Mall Galleries, London

1996
- International Art Show. World Trade Centre, Dubai, United Arab Emirates
- *Royal Academicians in Dubrovnik*. Royal Academy of Arts, London

1997
- *Works on Paper from the Royal Academy*. Art Museum, Sharjah, United Arab Emirates
- *Royal Academicians in Dubrovnik*. Royal Academy of Arts, London
- *Royal Academicians*. Dubrovnik City Art Gallery, Dubrovnik
- *The Print Show*. Concourse Gallery, Barbican Centre, London
- *New Orientalists*. Abu Dhabi Cultural Foundation, Abu Dhabi and Majlis Gallery, Dubai, United Arab Emirates
- Summer Exhibition. Royal Academy of Arts, London
- *The Railway Poster in Britain*. Tokyo Station Gallery, Japan

Commissions since 1981

1981　*Victoria Street, Amex House, Tolmer Square* commissioned by Elemeta Ltd

1982　*Speed* poster commissioned by British Rail

1983　*The Economist Building*, collection of The Economist

1984　*Hampton Court* commissioned by Building Design and presented to HRH The Prince of Wales

1985　*Wigan Reflections* commissioned by the Metropolitan Borough of Wigan
Billingsgate painting and print commissioned by Elemeta Ltd

1986　*Terminal 4* – four paintings commissioned by British Airports Authority for the Terminal 4 Building at Heathrow Airport
Pontiac commissioned by Gillette

1987　*Lloyd's* painting commissioned by Jardine and presented to Sir Peter Miller, Chairman

Cumbrian Landscape II book cover for Native Stones by David Craig (Secker and Warburg)

Lloyd's print, drawings, stencils and seritraces and working proof acquired by the Tate Gallery Archives, London. *Lloyd's* print acquired by the Tate Gallery

Dancing Reflections screenprint commissioned by the Hospital for Nervous Diseases

1988　*Plaza* screenprint commissioned by Anderson O'Day Gallery
Broadgate commissioned by Guildhall Museum

1989　*Water-Lily* commissioned by Uni-Life, Luxembourg
Kembrey Park and *Kembrey Trellis* paintings commissioned by Aukett Associates
No 6 Broadgate two paintings for the viewing area commissioned by Rosehaugh Plc

1990　*City Lights* screenprint commissioned by the Royal Society of Painters and Etchers for the Print Collectors Club

Cornice screenprint and *Target Façade* commissioned by Mallabars for Target International

London Kings Cross, York, Leeds, Newcastle, Edinburgh – series of five paintings commissioned by InterCity to celebrate the electrification of the Eastern Seaboard and the InterCity 225 service between London and Edinburgh

1991　*Cumulus* screenprint commissioned by Coriander Studio
Toltec Park painting commissioned by Sun Alliance for the main foyer of their Toltec Park building in Bristol

1992　*Toltec Sunset* screenprint for Aukett Associates and Sun Alliance
Lennox Wood painting commissioned by Aukett Associates. Image used for cover of company's 1991 annual report
Painting commissioned by Waters & Robson Ltd for Abbey Well Art Label soft drinks
Bath painting for poster commissioned by InterCity

1993　*Waterloo International* commissioned by Nicholas Grimshaw & Partners, YRM Anthony Hunt Associates, Sir Alexander Gibb & Partners, Davis Landon and Everest, J Roger Preston, Bovis Construction Ltd
Reading College commissioned by Reading College of Art & Technology
Brighton Pavilion commissioned by the University of Brighton
Shire Hall commissioned by Staffordshire County Council

1994　*Central* painting commissioned by InterCity
Westminster Reflected painting commissioned by InterCity
Great Western at Paddington painting commissioned by Great Western

1994-96　*Glenmorangie Still, Glencoe, Glenfinnan, Loch Shiel, Quiraing, Isle of Skye* and *Nevis Range* commissioned by ScotRail

1995　*Shoreditch Church* and *Waterloo International* commissioned by Hackney Community College
Loch Shiel and *Glencoe* silkscreen prints commissioned by Coriander Studio and The Redfern Gallery

1996　*Eros Piccadilly, Westminster* and *Taxis* paintings commissioned by Gatwick Express
Series of twelve plates to be produced at Limoges
St Augustine's Abbey painting commissioned by English Heritage
Western Isle commissioned by Coriander studio
Brookland Heights painting for Proctor and Gamble, commissioned by Aukett Associates
Christmas Candle commissioned by Chelsea Arts Club

1997　*Clockhouse Tower* commissioned by Aukett Associates
Dusk and Dawn – two Screenprints commissioned by Coriander Studio
Loughborough commissioned by Loughborough University
National Bank of Dubai – set of three paintings commissioned by the National Bank of Dubai

Publications and Bibliography

Brendan Neiland – Angela Flowers Gallery. Marina Vaizey (Financial Times), June 1970

Art in Britain. Edward Lucie-Smith (Thames and Hudson), 1970

Brendan Neiland - Graphics. Pat Gilmour (Arts Review), March 1970

Studio International - Exhibition review

London Letter. William Feaver (Art International), April 1972

Brendan Neiland - Traffic Jams. Marina Vaizey (Financial Times), March 1972

Graphics. Pat Gilmour (Arts Review), July 1973

Variazoni della Realta. Marina Vaizey (Financial Times), March 1972

The Other Careers. Joan Goodman & Mike Bygrave (Woodhouse Ltd), 1973

Skyscrapers. Victoria Radin (The Observer), September 1974

Exhibitions in Manchester. Mareta Bates (The Guardian), October 1974

Exhibition Review. Marina Vaizey (The Sunday Times), September 1974

Exhibition Review. James Faure-Walker (Studio International)

Reflections on a Building. (Building Design), October 1974

London Exhibitions. Fennella Creighton (Art International), November 1974

Exhibition Review. (Oxford Mail), June 1976

Painting and Prints by Brendan Neiland. (Yorkshire Post)

City Through the Distorting Glass. John Hewitt (Telegraph & Argus), February 1976

Brendan Neiland. Stephen Chaplin (Arts Review), February 1976

Exhibition Review. Marina Vaizey (The Sunday Times), June 1976

Brendan Neiland - Jordan Gallery Prints. Rosemary Simmons (Arts Review), June 1976

Realism Rules OK. Edward Lucie-Smith (Art & Artists), September 1976

Contemporary Artists. Colin Naylor & Genisis P Orridge (St James' Press), 1977

Brendan Neiland. Melanie Hart (Art Monthly), November 1979

Brendan Neiland. Marina Vaizey (Art International), November 1979

Brendan Neiland. Brian Wallworth (Arts Review), October 1979

Realism for All. Michael Shepherd (The Sunday Telegraph), October 1979

Brendan Neiland - Recent Paintings 1977-79. Edward Lucie-Smith (Fischer Fine Art Catalogue), October 1978

Contemporary British Artists. Edited by Charlotte Parry-Cooke (Bergstrom & Boyle Books), 1979

The Cool & the Celebratory. Deanna Petherbridge (Architectural Review), April 1980

Super Realism Painting & Sculpture. Christine Lindsay (Orbis Books), 1981

Artists in Print. Pat Gilmour (BBC Publications Ltd), 1981

Presences of Nature, Words and Images of the Lake District. Edited by Neil Hanson (Carlisle Museum & City Art Gallery), 1982

Artistry in Architecture. Janet Abrams (Building Design, Number 611), September 24, 1982

The Artist as Photographer. Marina Vaizey (Sedgewick & Jackson Ltd), 1982

Reflections on the Life of a Building. Susan Wolk (Building Design), 1984

A Study of Patronage. John Russell Taylor (The Times), January 10, 1984

A Study of Realism and All Very British. (The Sydney Morning Herald), October 1983

The Artefacts of Ideas. (Apollo), January 1984

How to Help The Artist. Marina Vaizey (The Sunday Times), October 28, 1984

Brendan Neiland. An appreciation by Marina Vaizey (Building Design), May 25, 1984

From Art School to Industry 1859-1986. A Brighton Polytechnic Publication

Educating for Art. Rod Taylor (Longman), 1986

Jardine Present Painting to Lloyd's. Briefing (A Lloyd's Publication), 1987

Brendan Neiland - Reflective Genius in a Pragmatic World. (Triangle – Lloyd's Staff Newspaper, Number 67), April 1987

Why 51 Artists Are Teaching Wigan a Lesson. Marina Vaizey (The Sunday Times), May 17, 1987

Reflections in an Urban Eye. Jane McCarthy (The Sunday Times Magazine), September 6, 1987

Brendan Neiland - Façades. Mary Rose Beaumont (Arts Review) September 25, 1987

Exhibition Review. Marina Vaizey (The Sunday Times), September 27, 1987

Look at Life. Marina Vaizey (Building Design), September 11, 1987

Brendan Neiland - Façades. Marina Vaizey (Catalogue introduction to exhibition at Fischer Fine Art Gallery)

London Galleries. William Packer (Financial Times), September 10, 1987

A Sunday Stroll Inspires Brendan. (Lloyd's Magazine), September 1987

Brendan Neiland – Fischer Fine Art. Fiona Dunlop – Interview Artline (International Art News, Vol. 3, No 9), 1987

The Brendan Neiland Exhibition. (The Architect), September 1987

Perspective. (Building Design, No 923), February 1989

City Lights. (Building Design, No 924), February 1989

Painting beyond Architecture. Colin Amery (RIBA Journal), February 1989

The Whitworth Art Gallery – The First Hundred Years, Lloyd's 1986. Sarah Hyde, February 1989

The Inspiration of Landscape – Artists in National Parks. Brian Redhead (Phaidon Books)

1990 Chelsea Arts Club Yearbook

Royal Academy Illustrated

Playing to the Seasonal Gallery. Review by Marina Vaizey (The Sunday Times), June, 9, 1991

Artist Oils the Wheels. Article by Ross Kaniuk (The Evening Standard)

Brendan Neiland. Reinhard Rudolph, William Packer & Marina Vaizey (Fischer Fine Art illustrated catalogue)

Exhibitions. Editor Paul Finch (Building Design, Number 1050), September 27, 1991

Critics Choice. (The Times), October 4, 1991

Brendan Neiland RE in Conversation with Michael Spender. (Water Colours Drawings and Prints, Vol 6, No 4)

First Class Traveller Brendan Neiland. Tony Quinn (Summer Issue of InterCity Magazine), 1992

The New Patrons. (Christies' special exhibition catalogue), 1992

Approaching Art & Design. Rod Taylor (Longman)

Visual Arts in Education. Rod Taylor (Falmer Press)

InterCity Magazine, September 1992

Interview with Bryan Edmundson. (Catalogue of Drumcroon Exhibition), 1992

The Artist's View: Commissioned Art & Professional Practice – handbook to be used with video. Brendan Neiland

Brendan Neiland, New Paintings. Roger de Grey, 1993

The Recent Work of Brendan Neiland, New Paintings. William Packer, 1993

Listening to the Light – The Art of Brendan Neiland, New Paintings. Michael Tucker, 1993

Brendan Neiland: Painter, Printmaker, A Display of Prints and Working Materials. Nicholas Savage, 1994

Reflections on Printmaking with Brendan Neiland, A Display of Prints and Working Materials. Brad Faine

What's On magazine (No 212), United Arab Emirates, 1996

Rashid School News, March 1996

Horizons (Issue 16), April-May 1996

The Herald, April 3, 1996

Publications and Bibliography [cont.]

The Sunday Times (Ecosse Section 11), April 28, 1996

The Oban Times, May 2, 1996

Modern Railways, May 1996

Design Week, April 1996

Royal Academy of Arts' Summer Exhibition Review, June 1996

Printmaking Today – Brendan Neiland RA Interview with Rosemary
Simmons (Vol 6, No 1)

What's On magazine (No 219), October 1996

The Art of Business and the Business in Art. (Man in the Gulf magazine) January-
February 1997

Whoops, RA commits a new Hanging Offence. Robin Stringer (Evening Standard),
June 10, 1997

Few Surprises, Some Delights. Richard Dorment (The Daily Telegraph),
May 28, 1997

The Sunday Observer, William Feaver, June 15

Television, Radio and Video

Big Paintings for Public Places. (BBC Television), 1969

Far To Go. Brendan Neiland Talking to Hugh Macpherson

Artists in Print - Lithography. Produced by Suzanne Davis (BBC Television), March 1981

Celebration - Wigan Print Extravaganza. (Granada Television), June 1987

Wide Angle. (Anglia Television), 1992

Third Eye. (BBC Radio 3), 1992

Now Showing. Directed by Alan Velecky (BBC), March 14, 1993

Brendan Neiland Commissioned Art and Professional Practice. Directed by Gavin
Nettleton (University of Brighton)

Screen Printing with Water-Based Inks. Directed by Gavin Nettleton
(University of Brighton), 1995

Portrait of an Artist. Directed by Sam Docherty (Delphic Production), 1996

Interview for Nevis Radio with Gina Kennedy, 1996

Public Lectures

Buildings Within Buildings - Reflections on Paintings. Royal Institute of British
Architects, London 1989

The Working Artist. Royal Academy of Arts, London 1994

Paintings Commissions and Prints. Whitworth Art Gallery, London 1995

The Artist at Work. University College, London 1996

Prints and Paintings. Pallant House, Chichester

On Reflection, The Making of an Artist. Inaugural Lecture (University of Brighton), 1997

Public Collections

Arts Council of Great Britain

Victoria & Albert Museum

Gulbenkian Foundation

Toronto Art Gallery

Brooklyn Museum, USA

Graves Art Gallery, Sheffield

Department of the Environment

Bradford City Art Gallery

Rochdale Art Gallery

Fitzwilliam Museum, Cambridge

Leicester Education Authority

West Riding of Yorkshire County Council

Ford Collection, Great Britain

Leicester Museum & Art Gallery

Leigh Museum & Art Gallery

South London Art Gallery

Glasgow Museum & Art Gallery

Bolton Museum & Art Gallery

Southampton Museum & Art Gallery

Carlisle Museum & Art Gallery

Towner Art Gallery, Eastbourne

Government Art Collection

The Tate Gallery, London

The Contemporary Art Society

Boston Museum of Fine Art, USA

Birmingham City Art Gallery

Rutherstone Collection, Manchester

Whitworth Art Gallery, Manchester

Salford University

Brunel University

Cleveland Museum

Museum of London

Elemeta Collection

Dudley Museum

Drumcroon Gallery, Wigan

Portsmouth City Museum

Leeds City Art Gallery

Sheffield University

Wiltshire Museum Services

Guildhall Museum, City of London

Staffordshire County Council

Brighton University

European Parliament, Brussels

Reading College of Arts & Technology

Hackney Community College

The Royal College of Art

The Open University

University of Northumbria

The British Embassy, Paris

Loughborough University

English Heritage

List of Paintings

Acknowledgements

Whilst compiling this book was only a matter of months, its subject matter has occupied the best part of my life and I have received support and encouragement from many exceptional people. In particular, I would like to thank The Redfern Gallery – Maggie Thornton, Richard Selby and particularly Richard Gault, my agents and friends; not forgetting the support in the beginning of Angela Flowers, Wolfgang Fischer and Gordon Samuel; Brad Faine and Larry Gibilaro for their friendship and positive criticism; John Thake and Andrew Lett of Aukett for their confidence; Ian Hurst for his great ideas and sense of humour; Jonathan Towle of Paul Smith for his impeccable taste; Jane Priestman for her support and help; Martyn Cornwall for his lively encouragement; Bill Packer for many animated discussions in France; Marina Vaizey whose support has meant so much to me; Stan Smith, a friend and fellow traveller; Sid Rose for first bringing me out to the Middle East; The University of Brighton and, especially, Professors David Watson, Director and Bruce Brown, Dean, for all their support and not least their patience; Ian Potts and Chubb Harrison, friends and artists; my two daughters Naomi and Lucy; Janet Fleming whose support and friendship cover many years; Chris Green and Rob Mason from InterCity onwards; Alie Mayne, Tessa Carr and James Robinson of the Royal Academy of Arts, always cheerful, friendly and incredibly supportive; Roger Jupe for timely criticism; Mike Ashton with whom it is a pleasure to work; Katy Taylor for her fun, liveliness and research; Peter Ridgway for his foresight and belief; Rob Hersey, whose help I have appreciated greatly; Jonathan Stone for his encouragement; Nick Savage of the Royal Academy of Arts for looking after my prints so well; Catherine Demangeot, Dejan Vrbanovic and Kate John of Motivate Publishing for their patience, calmness and big brains, and Ian Fairservice for his enthusiasm and encouragement; Cathy Courtney who was skilful enough to get the best out of me; and all those individuals and corporations whose commissions have helped me in the pursuance of my art.

My very special thanks to a very special person – Hilary.

Last but not least, I would like to thank the National Bank of Dubai, and particularly Abdullah Saleh and Fraser McKenzie, whose sponsorship support made possible the publication of this book.